"One of the greatest scandals besetting the higher education sector worldwide is that even as tuition fees rocket, the position of those teaching becomes less secure and less formally legitimised... This important book lays out the detail of this state of affairs... In a brilliant analysis, Bérubé demonstrates the fallacy of establishing some specific standard of cognitive capacity as normative, and uses that to show that the humanities, unlike all conservative positions, are concerned firmly with the extensions of thinking and the disruptions that that brings... Bérubé and his co-author Jennifer Ruth follow through the logic of a condition in which the majority of teaching is done by the new academic precariat. Their logic is laid out with exemplary clarity and with impressive factual detail."

— Thomas Docherty, *Times Higher Education*

"Finally, a book that defends the humanities not with violins but rather by linking them to the status of contingent labor in the academy, and what the deplorable state of both means for all of us. *The Humanities, Higher Education and Academic Freedom* is an important intervention that spotlights the most salient defense of tenure for our times. Bérubé and Ruth center on the forgotten side of academic freedom, namely governance. This is a bracing and necessary book that should be mandatory reading for all department chairs—and everyone else who teaches college."

— Leonard Cassuto, Professor of English,
Fordham University, and columnist for
The Chronicle of Higher Education

"The Humanities are fine. The profession of teaching the Humanities, on the other hand, is a disaster. Rather than offering just another woeful dirge on American higher education, Bérubé and Ruth detail the distinct choices that have led us into this mess and chart a pragmatic course to build a new, sustainable, future."

— David Perry, Associate Professor of English,
Dominican University

"If I was one of the usual stable of writers asked to churn out op-eds on the decline of humanities, I would steer well clear of this book. It makes accepted opinion on these issues look really, really dumb. It shows brilliantly and conclusively that the loudly-trumpeted crisis of the humanities is really a crisis of university employment, not of trendy ideas. The book ought to be required reading for anyone who cares about ideas or for that matter expects professionalism from the university. This wake-up call should not be necessary. But a lot of opinion-makers have been asleep at the switch."

— Bruce Robbins, Old Dominion Foundation Professor
in the Humanities, Columbia University

"This witty and ferocious defense of the American university not only shows how the attacks on the humanities, assaults on academic freedom, and decimation of the tenure-line professoriate have worked together – all in the name of corporatization and budgetary "efficiency" – to bring this once proud institution to its knees, but also demands that the few remaining tenure-line faculty stop rationalizing these changes, and bestir themselves to resist them."

— Karen Kelsky, Academic Job Market Consultant
and Founder of 'The Professor Is In'

"Innovative solutions are out there, solutions that propose reforming the largely arbitrary way that many departments go about acquiring contingent labor. Michael Bérubé and Jennifer Ruth argue in their book, *The Humanities, Higher Education, and Academic Freedom: Three Necessary Arguments*, forthcoming in May from Palgrave Macmillan, that departments should develop teaching-intensive tenure tracks. The search protocols and evaluation processes we've long used for conventional tenure-track faculty can be adapted for teaching-intensive positions."

— Emily E. VanDette, *The Chronicle of Higher Education*

Also by Michael Bérubé

THE AESTHETICS OF CULTURAL STUDIES (*ed.*)

THE EMPLOYMENT OF ENGLISH: Theory, Jobs, and the Future of Literary Studies

HIGHER EDUCATION UNDER FIRE: Politics, Economics, and the Crisis of The Humanities (*ed.*)

THE LEFT AT WAR

WHAT'S LIBERAL ABOUT THE LIBERAL ARTS?

LIFE AS WE KNOW IT: A Father, a Family, and an Exceptional Child

MARGINAL FORCES / CULTURAL CENTERS: Tolson, Pynchon, and the Politics of the Canon

PUBLIC ACCESS: Literary Theory and American Cultural Politics

RHETORICAL OCCASIONS: Essays on Humans and the Humanities

Also by Jennifer Ruth

NOVEL PROFESSIONS: Interested Disinterest and the Making of the Professional in the Victorian Novel

The Humanities, Higher Education, and Academic Freedom
Three Necessary Arguments

Michael Bérubé
Professor of Literature, Pennsylvania State University, USA

and

Jennifer Ruth
Associate Professor in English, Portland State University, USA

© 2015 Michael Bérubé and Jennifer Ruth

All rights reserved. No reproduction, copy or transmission of this publication may be made without written permission.

No portion of this publication may be reproduced, copied or transmitted save with written permission or in accordance with the provisions of the Copyright, Designs and Patents Act 1988, or under the terms of any licence permitting limited copying issued by the Copyright Licensing Agency, Saffron House, 6–10 Kirby Street, London EC1N 8TS.

Any person who does any unauthorized act in relation to this publication may be liable to criminal prosecution and civil claims for damages.

The authors have asserted their rights to be identified as the authors of this work in accordance with the Copyright, Designs and Patents Act 1988.

First published 2015 by
PALGRAVE MACMILLAN

Palgrave Macmillan in the UK is an imprint of Macmillan Publishers Limited, registered in England, company number 785998, of Houndmills, Basingstoke Hampshire RG21 6XS.

Palgrave Macmillan in the US is a division of St Martin's Press LLC, 175 Fifth Avenue, New York, NY 10010.

Palgrave Macmillan is the global academic imprint of the above companies and has companies and representatives throughout the world.

Palgrave® and Macmillan® are registered trademarks in the United States, the United Kingdom, Europe and other countries.

ISBN 978–1–137–50610–8   hardback
ISBN 978–1–137–50611–5   paperback

This book is printed on paper suitable for recycling and made from fully managed and sustained forest sources. Logging, pulping and manufacturing processes are expected to conform to the environmental regulations of the country of origin.

A catalogue record for this book is available from the British Library.

A catalog record for this book is available from the Library of Congress.

Typeset by MPS Limited, Chennai, India.

Contents

List of Figures vi
Acknowledgments vii
Introduction: This is Not the Crisis You're Looking For 1
Michael Bérubé and Jennifer Ruth
1 Value and Values 27
 Michael Bérubé
2 Slow Death and Painful Labors 57
 Jennifer Ruth
3 From Professionalism to Patronage 87
 Jennifer Ruth and Michael Bérubé
4 On the Rails 121
 Jennifer Ruth and Michael Bérubé
Appendix: Implementing a Teaching-Intensive
Tenure Track at Portland State University 142
Bibliography 149
Index 157

List of Figures

1	Humanities degrees boomed as a percentage of all degrees in the 1960s	4
2	Humanities degrees as a percentage of the American college-age population	6

Acknowledgments

Jennifer: I want to thank Michael for inviting me to write this book with him. It has been a pleasure from start to finish. I also want to thank Amy Greenstadt and Michele Glazer. The worst heartbreak of academic life has been worth the rock-solid, lifelong friendship we forged. I thank Renee Honn and Tiffany Kraft for having taught me much about adjunctification and, in general, being wise and wonderful human beings. Lastly, I'd like to thank Michael Meranze and Chris Newfield for their encouraging support of my contributions to *Remaking the University*. Important parts of this book originated there.

Michael: I want to thank Jennifer for writing to me and rousing me from some dogmatic slumbers. It became clear to me, after a few weeks' correspondence, that she is one of the very few people who are thinking clearly and honestly about how the profession of college teaching has been deprofessionalized, and with what consequences. (I was not thinking altogether clearly about these things myself, despite having thought about them for 20 years.) And I'd like to join Jennifer in thanking Michael Meranze and Chris Newfield—for their own work on these matters, and for their encouraging support of Jennifer's contributions to *Remaking the University*. When I read her posts, I knew I had to ask her to write this book with me.

Portions of the introduction have previously appeared in *Inside Higher Ed* and the *Chronicle of Higher Education*; a snippet of Chapter 1 was published in *Cognitive Disability and its Challenge to Moral Philosophy*, edited by Eva Feder Kittay and Licia Carlson (Wiley-Blackwell, 2010).

Introduction: This is Not the Crisis You're Looking For

Michael Bérubé and Jennifer Ruth

It has become an iron law of American journalism that no one is permitted to write the word "humanities" in a sentence that does not also include the word "decline." Case in point: in the summer of 2013 the American Academy of Arts and Sciences released a report, *The Heart of the Matter*, that sought to promote the humanities and social sciences as important objects of study alongside the STEM disciplines (science, technology, engineering, and mathematics), and more generally as part of a kind of American civic nationalism. What followed the release of that rather mild report was an almost surreal series of newspaper articles about the decline of the humanities, as if *that* had been the subject of the report. The general consensus was this: undergraduates have voted with their feet. Humanities professors have killed interest in their own disciplines, and declining student enrollments are the proof. In the words of David Brooks, *New York Times* columnist and member of the committee that produced the AAAS report, "the humanities are not only being bulldozed by an unforgiving job market. They are committing suicide because many humanists have lost faith in their own enterprise."[1]

Brooks's account was but one version of a narrative that has dominated discussion of the humanities for over two decades. "A half-century ago, 14 percent of college degrees were awarded to people who majored in the humanities," Brooks wrote. "Today, only 7 percent of graduates in the country are humanities majors." The reason for the dramatic drop-off is that the humanities took up trendy and ephemeral matters, becoming "less about the old notions of truth, beauty and goodness and more about political and social categories like race, class and gender.... To the earnest 19-year-old with lofty dreams of self-understanding and moral greatness, the humanities in this guise were bound to seem less consequential and more boring."

Likewise, in his 2009 *American Scholar* essay, "The Decline of the English Department," William M. Chace, then the president of Emory University, noted that English accounted for 7.6 percent of all bachelor's degrees in 1970–71, but only 3.9 percent in 2003–4. "If nothing is done to put an end to the process of disintegration, the numbers will continue in a steady downward spiral," he warned.[2] In 2013, in the *Chronicle of Higher Education*, Emory English professor Mark Bauerlein cited similar numbers, concluding, "English has gone from a major unit in the university to a minor one."[3] In November 2010, MSNBC anchor Tamron Hall remarked with alarm that "students wanting to take up majors like art history and literature are now making the jump to more-specialized fields like business and economics, and it's getting worse."[4] A chart appeared on-screen. "Just look at this," Hall said. "In 2007 just 8 percent of bachelor's degrees were given to disciplines in the humanities." In 1966 that figure had been 17.4 percent.

So everyone knows why tenure-track jobs have dried up and funds have evaporated: students have abandoned the humanities in droves. There's only one problem with those insistent accounts of the decline of the humanities in undergraduate education: they are wrong. Factually, stubbornly, determinedly wrong. As it happens, there was a decline in bachelor's degrees in English, just as there was a drop-off in humanities enrollments more generally. But it happened almost entirely between 1970 and 1980. It is old news. Students are not "now making the jump" to other fields, and it is not "getting worse." It is not a "recent shift." There is no "steady downward spiral." It is more like the sales of Beatles records—huge in the 1960s, then dropping off sharply in the 1970s.

And why does that matter? Because many of the accounts of the decline of the humanities are tendentious, and they continue to distract attention from the *real* crisis. Even when they are ostensibly couched as defenses of study in the humanities, as Brooks's column is, they are attacks on current practices in the humanities—like the study of race, class, gender, and other boring things.[5] Or the rise of "theory." Or the study of popular culture. Or the preponderance of jargon. Or the fragmentation of the curriculum. Or your colleague down the hall, whose work you never liked and who is probably undermining the English major as you type. But most of the things blamed for the decline in enrollments happened *after* the decline in enrollments had stopped. Theory, race/gender/class/sexuality, jargon, popular culture ... these things were hard to find in humanities departments in the 1970s. They became part of the fabric in our end of campus in the 1980s and 1990s.

And then a funny thing happened in the 1980s and 1990s: enrollments crept back up a bit. Weirdly, no one at the time seemed to take any solace in this. All through those decades, people kept churning out essays about the decline and fall of English and the humanities. "In 1970 we were the biggest thing on campus," we said. "We earned our swagger. Everybody jumped back when a humanist walked by." *Seven point six percent of all degrees!* Bliss was it in that dawn to be alive. Nobody stopped and looked at the numbers more closely. No one took 1980 as a starting point instead of 1970. For that matter, no one pointed out that 1970 was a blip, an anomaly, a high-water mark that represented a swift and unprecedented boom in humanities enrollments (see Figure 1).

Today, even when someone acknowledges that blip, they *still* tell a story of constant decline. Thus Chace admits that from the late 1940s to 1970, English majors climbed from 17,000 to 64,000; "but by 1985/86," he concludes, "the number of undergraduate English majors had fallen back to 34,000, despite a hefty increase in total nationwide undergraduate enrollment."

The Humanities, Higher Education, and Academic Freedom

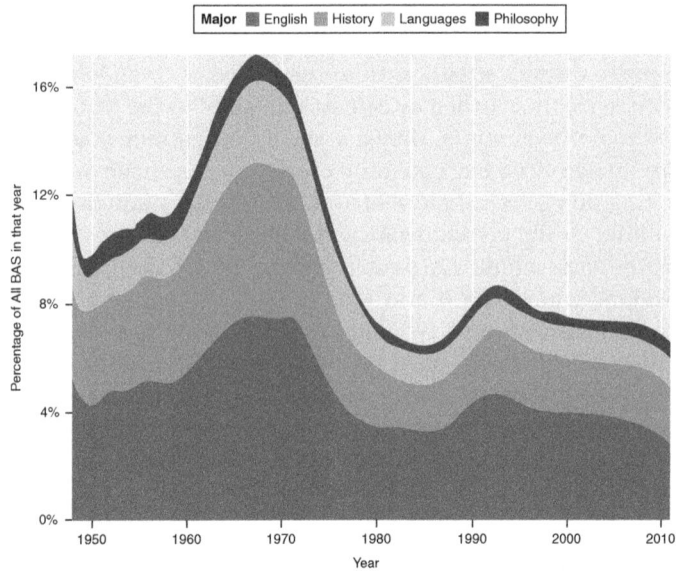

Figure 1 Humanities degrees boomed as a percentage of all degrees in the 1960s

Quite true. But by 2003–4, when Chace lamented that English accounted for only 3.9 percent of bachelor's degrees, that number was 54,000—and he did not acknowledge as much. Why was no one writing about how the number of English majors grew by 20,000 over 20 years—almost a 60 percent increase?

Because the underlying lament is almost always about recent intellectual developments in the humanities, and the pre-cooked enrollment numbers are nothing more than a pretext for jeremiads. Thus in his 1999 *New York Review of Books* essay, titled (what else?) "The Decline and Fall of Literature," Andrew Delbanco wrote: "Lately it has become impossible to say with confidence whether such topics as 'Eat Me; Captain Cook and the Ingestion of the Other' or 'The Semiotics of Sinatra' are parodies of what goes on [at the annual MLA convention] or serious presentations by credentialed scholars."[6] Is it really so impossible, for a reasonably informed reader? The first title is from a work of fiction, a sendup of academe and its inhabitants. It is a very silly title. The second title is real—and not silly at all. On the contrary, "the semiotics of Sinatra" should sound like an entirely plausible topic to anyone who knows anything about the history of twentieth-century American popular culture. But then, in the 1990s it was never quite clear why so many distinguished critics had such trouble with topics most people would find wholly unobjectionable—as when Frank Kermode complained, in a 1997 essay in the *Atlantic Monthly*, about papers on such outlandish subjects as "the gendering of popular morality in certain nineteenth-century novels, the cultural politics of domesticity in a novel by Harriet Beecher Stowe, Mother in the Holocaust, Toni Morrison's feminized historical epic, and so forth."[7] One would have thought that literature, and literary study, was capacious enough to include such things—and that a critic as accomplished as Kermode would have been able to tolerate the notion.

Fortunately, Nate Silver, the statistician who has become famous for the accuracy of his analyses of polling data, weighed in on the inexorable decline of the humanities, and found that "the relative decline of majors like English is modest when accounting for the increased propensity of Americans to go to college." Silver elaborated: "In fact, the number of new degrees in English is fairly similar to what it has been for most of the last 20 years as a share of the college-age population. In 2011, 1.1 out of every 100 21-year-olds graduated with a bachelor's degree in English, down only incrementally from 1.2 in 2001 and 1.3 in 1991. And the percentage of English majors as a share of the population is actually higher than it was in 1981, when only 0.7 out of every 100 21-year-olds received a degree in English."[8] In a similar vein, Ben Schmidt showed in a *Chronicle of Higher Education* essay that the numbers get even more interestingly murky when you correlate them to the college-age population *and* extend them before 1967 (see Figure 2):

> "percentage of all degrees" is a strange denominator. Taking into account the massive changes in the American university since the Second World War, it's the resilience of the humanities that should be surprising. If you care about humanistic education, you shouldn't be worrying about market share *inside the university*. You should care about the whole population. And while the 60s boom still stands out, we give out far more population-normalized degrees in the humanities now than we did in the 1950s or the 1980s.[9]

The argument is all the stronger for the visual and performing arts, though it is never made; the assumption, apparently,

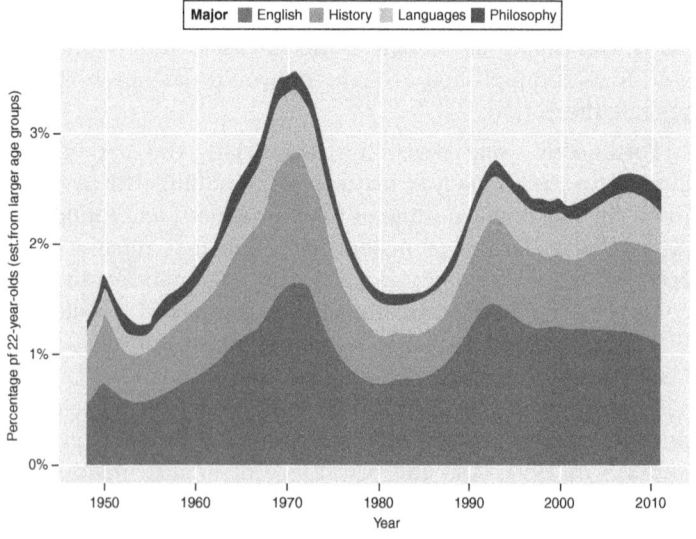

Figure 2 Humanities degrees as a percentage of the American college-age population

is that when SUNY-Albany announced program closures in French, Italian, Russian, Classics, and Theater in 2010, it was simply a harbinger of things to come, a selloff of dying and useless fields. But if you look at the Digest of Education Statistics, published annually by the National Center for Education Statistics (and referenced almost never by the "decline chorus"), you will find an extraordinary thing: in 1970, out of 839,730 undergraduate degrees, 30,394 were awarded in the visual and performing arts. By 2011–12 (the most recent year for which figures are available as we go to press), the number of overall degrees had more than doubled, to 1,791,046—but the number of degrees in the visual and performing arts had more than *tripled*, to 95,797. And yet, somehow, no one has noticed this. Obviously we must cut programs in dance and sculpture—they don't contribute to the GDP, and nobody is taking those courses anyway.

It is true that there are individual institutions that have experienced recent enrollment declines in the humanities. One of the reports that sparked national discussion in 2013, for instance, was issued by Harvard—showing a decline in humanities "concentrators" from 21 percent to 17 percent over the period 2003–12. (That report also starts off, remarkably enough, by noting that "between 1966 and 2010, Bachelor's Degree Completions in the Humanities halved nationwide, falling from 14 to 7% of all degrees taken." As always, 1966 is the loaded-dice starting point.[10]) And in a 2013 *New York Times* article, Verlyn Klinkenborg reported that "in 1991, 165 students graduated from Yale with a B.A. in English literature. By 2012, that number was 62. In 1991, the top two majors at Yale were history and English. In 2013, they were economics and political science."[11] For people who are inclined to take Harvard and Yale as representative of American higher education in general, these are surely alarming numbers.

But overall, the real narrative should go something like this: despite skyrocketing tuition rates and the rise of the predatory student-loan industry; despite all the ritual handwringing by disgruntled professors and the occasional op-ed hit man; despite decades' worth of rhetoric about how either (a) fields like art history and literature are elite, niche-market affairs that will render students unemployable, or (b) students are abandoning the humanities because they are callow, market-driven careerists; *despite all of that*, undergraduate enrollments in the humanities have held relatively steady since 1980 (in relation to all degree holders, and in relation to the larger age cohort), and undergraduate enrollments in the arts and humanities combined are almost precisely where they were in 1970.

Just as important, while all that was going on, the disciplines of the humanities responded to the world around them. *Mirabile dictu*, it turns out that race, class, and gender are actually matters of interest to millions of undergraduates, and queer theory, disability studies, and science studies have widened the purview of the humanities while enriching the graduate and undergraduate curriculum. None of this has sidelined any talk about truth, beauty, or goodness—but, rather, to the consternation of many conservatives (and many intellectually conservative liberals), it has complicated our notions of truth, beauty, and goodness precisely by bringing more voices into the discussion of such matters.

Indeed, as Christopher Newfield argues in *Unmaking the Public University*, that was the point of the culture wars of the 1990s: to attack and delegitimate "the study of race, gender, and sexuality, the humanities fields that did the bulk of the research and teaching in these fields, the students of color who seemed to benefit from them, and the universities that harbored all of these."[12] In retrospect (and as some of us correctly argued at the time), the culture wars on campus were not distractions from the right's economic agenda, the agenda of privatization and of deep cuts in support for public universities; the two strategies worked hand in hand. As Newfield has it,

> Privatization has systematically diminished the public university's distinctive features. One of these was top quality at a

low cost to the individual student and his or her family. The result of this synthesis was freedom to choose a field of study without overriding awareness of its future income potential. A further result was graduation with little to no debt, allowing the graduate from a low-income background to have the same shot as others at the freedom to take poorly paying but satisfying work, or a shot at international travel, or a shot at being a professional painter or dancer.[13]

Newfield is right about the culture wars, and right about privatization; the only thing missing from his otherwise brilliant analysis of how the defunding of public universities constituted an assault on the American middle class is an acknowledgment that despite it all, undergraduates keep dreaming of being professional painters and dancers, as the numbers of majors in the fine and performing arts show us. It is odd, is it not? Why, one would almost be tempted to conclude that the arts—and, to a lesser degree, the humanities—have some intellectual, creative, and emotional power after all.

And so the obvious question asserts itself: if the numbers are so much less alarming than we've been led to believe, why do scholars and teachers in the humanities continue to talk—persistently, strenuously, even obsessively—in terms of "crisis"?

There are two reasons, we think. One is that there are plenty of scholars and teachers in the humanities who have been inured to the idea that they are being systemically ignored, misunderstood, and/or devalued. This is understandable enough; they walk across campus and see the gleaming new Business Administration building, the sparkling, beautifully equipped Center for Nanotechnology and Advanced Bioengineering, and the gorgeous new stadium, arena, and student activity center—and then they trudge into their ancient cubicle in the dilapidated, un-air-conditioned Arts and Humanities Building, and they grumble to themselves about campus priorities. Or, depending on their temperament, they take a perverse comfort in their place at the bottom of the funding food chain, telling themselves that people just don't appreciate the finer things in life, such as the study of the monuments and artifacts of human civilization—worth more, ultimately, than any amount of filthy lucre or creature comforts. These people are a ready audience for the "decline of the humanities" narrative, because it confirms for them what they are already wont to believe: they are surrounded by philistines, Know-Nothings, and annoying businessmen from Porlock.

For most professors, though, it is not resentment or self-pity that makes the decline narrative so compelling. It is the fact that the narrative *feels right*, inasmuch as it attempts to account for the pervasive, sinking feeling that something is very much amiss. Among humanities professors and graduate students, there is a keen sense that even if there is no immediate crisis of undergraduate enrollment, there nonetheless is a crisis. It is a crisis of graduate education and professional employment, and though it is not confined to the humanities—it is now endemic to higher education in general—it is often felt to be most pronounced in the humanities. It is also, relatedly, a crisis of funding, of prestige, and of legitimation. And whether this crisis is experienced as disorganized malaise or diamond-tipped rage depends largely on the person's employment situation. Because the crisis is not one of disappearing students. It is one of disappearing tenure-track jobs. Too many people have been snookered into thinking that the jobs disappeared because the students did; we have written this book to put that canard to rest once and for all.

* * *

We believe ours is something more than the standard-issue "defense" of the humanities, or of the liberal arts tradition in higher education more generally (which would of course include the physical and social sciences—everything that is not a narrowly designed "vocational" program). The book is partly that, particularly in the following chapter, but we think there are enough of those out there. Helen Small's *The Value of the Humanities*, to take one example, offers a painstakingly careful and measured assessment of the genre. We believe that the real crisis is that the profession of college teaching has been drastically deprofessionalized over the past 40 years, and that college teachers need to find ways of making this case to the general public—without suggesting that the legions of teachers off the tenure track are not doing professional-quality teaching. We want to explain to people who may not know what a provost is, or who don't use the word "decanal" in conversation, what *this* crisis looks like.

So what are these "three necessary arguments" of our subtitle? They go something like this. The first two are familiar in some precincts of the academy, but not all—and very rarely get an adequate hearing outside. The third is wholly unacknowledged, and sheds new and disturbing light on the first two.

One, the humanities are in fine shape, insofar as their intellectual value is concerned. We don't agree with every last thing every single person in the humanities has written or said over the past 40 years, but on the whole, the disciplines of the humanities are home to exciting and ambitious work in both emerging and traditional fields.

Two, while all this exciting and ambitious work has been going on, the profession of college teaching has been hollowed out as full-time, tenure-track positions have been converted to highly precarious positions (both full-time and part-time) that offer no possibility of tenure—which means, basically, all the job security of Wal-Mart or McDonald's.

Three, the deprofessionalization of college teaching has had consequences with which no one has fully come to terms—in academe or out. These consequences have unsettling implications for the future of graduate programs and for the mundane but important business of running academic departments. They are complex and contradictory and hard to fix, and we will elaborate on them in Chapters 2 and 3; suffice it to say here that massive hiring off the tenure track has effectively foregone systems of professional review for college faculty.

Here's how these three arguments came together. In the middle of the summer of 2013, as I was wading through the latest spate of decline-of-the-humanities essays, Jennifer wrote to me on what might seem to be an unrelated matter: a policy statement from the American Association of University Professors, recommending that all "contingent" faculty (we will explain the terminology, which is surprisingly complicated; for now we will use "contingent" to designate everyone not on the tenure track) be included in campus governance. The policy is a strong attempt to address a dire situation: at many universities, contingent faculty have no say whatsoever in any aspect of the way their departments or campuses are governed, so they are subject to potentially capricious hiring (and firing) practices. However, as Jennifer pointed out, since we are talking about faculty who effectively have no academic freedom—who can be punished or fired for any reason, usually without recourse to appeal or review—it is problematic to argue that they should serve on committees where their opinions and comments may well alienate the person or persons who hired them. Jennifer knew that I am an advocate for the rights of contingent faculty, and that (alongside my interest in disability studies) I focused my year as president of the Modern Language Association on their working conditions—even though the president of the MLA, and the MLA more generally, has nothing more than a bully pulpit when it comes to the working conditions of contingent faculty.

This conversation was punctuated by a series of essays that Jennifer wrote for the well-regarded academic blog *Remaking the University*, run by Michael Meranze and Christopher Newfield.[14] And at some point, I realized that I was corresponding with a former department chair who had actually reversed the trend toward the casualization of academic labor in her own department; who had successfully fought for tenure-track lines and successfully undone some of the under-the-table deals enjoyed by some of her faculty; and who was writing important essays about the experience. Asking her to co-author this book was an easy call.

For the most part, my experience has been that of an advocate in national organizations, though I have worked on my own workplace, as well. I helped rewrite the bylaws of the Penn State English department not long after my arrival in 2001, to ensure that our non-tenure-track faculty could not be capriciously demoted or fired, and that they had recourse to regular reviews as well as an appeal process when they disagreed with a review. I also serve on the Faculty Senate at Penn State, having been elected in 2012. But other than that, my experiences in this wing of academe consist mostly of my work with the national AAUP, leading two investigations of universities closing programs and firing tenured faculty, and writing a report on the role of the faculty in conditions of financial exigency. And, of course, writing essays and giving talks about the state of the humanities. Jennifer, by contrast, has done the critical but almost always invisible work of running a department, negotiating with deans and provosts, coming to terms with the stubborn fact that we have evolved a two- or three-tier hiring system in academe: one tier involves national searches, careful vetting processes, and rigorous peer review. The other two are almost entirely ad hoc, involving short- and long-term contingent faculty hired (and fired) almost any old way. The short-term faculty are often referred to as "adjuncts," and we will employ that designation here, differentiating them from the long-term, full-time faculty off the tenure track—but considering both groups as "contingent" faculty.

Jennifer and I decided on the following division of labor: we each would write on the state of the profession as we have seen and experienced it. Sometimes our voices are combined, and sometimes they are distinct. We hope that for the most part, *who* is talking *when* will be clear and that the pronoun shifts are not distracting. (The order of our names below the chapter titles in the Introduction, Chapters 3 and 4 shows who wrote most of it. Michael wrote Chapter 1 solo and Jennifer wrote Chapter 2. In Chapter 4, we hand the baton back and forth, and indicate when we are doing so.) Before we get to the nuts and bolts of what has gone wrong in the academic labor system—and how to set about fixing it—I take one more chapter to address the actual substance of work in the humanities in the past few decades. Too often, when I have rebutted the enrollment argument, I have been met with complaints that the numbers aren't really the point—the point is the sorry state of humanities departments in the United States, filled as they are with second-rate ideologues and incomprehensible cliques. I do not want that complaint to go unaddressed, not least because I have a visceral intolerance for second-rate ideologues and incomprehensible cliques. I just don't agree that American humanities departments are filled with them. I do, however, agree that the explicitly political attacks on humanities departments, over the past few decades, have helped to delegitimate new work in the humanities—precisely as they were designed to do. We then concentrate on the crisis of deprofessionalization—what it looks like from the inside, what it means for higher education, and how we can begin to turn it around. Chapter 2 is Jennifer's, and everything else is both of us, with some single-voiced sections scattered throughout. The Appendix consists of recommendations Jennifer and her colleague Amy Greenstadt have proposed for transitioning Portland State to a majority tenure-track professoriate, and that we think can be generalized well beyond Portland State.

Now a few words about what we hope to do in this book and why. The employment situation in academe is this: contingent-faculty members now make up over one million of the 1.5 million people teaching in American colleges and universities—about 70 percent of all faculty. Many of them are working at or under the poverty line, with an average salary of about $2700 per course, without health insurance; some of them, as the *Chronicle of Higher Education* reported in 2012, are living on food stamps.[15] These faculty members have no academic freedom worthy of the name, because they can be fired at will; and, when fired, many remain ineligible for unemployment benefits, because institutions routinely invoke the "reasonable assurance of continued employment" clause in federal unemployment law even for faculty members on yearly contracts who have no reasonable assurance of anything.

In 1970, the situation was reversed: more than 70 percent of college professors had tenure. Since then, ever-increasing numbers of students have been taught by an ever-decreasing number of tenured faculty. *That* is the real story of the relation between student enrollments and faculty jobs, and the numbers are staggering. In 1947—the good old days, before race, class, and gender ruined everything—there were 2.3 million undergraduates enrolled in American colleges and universities. In 1972, that number was 9.2 million. That 25-year period after World War II is widely understood as an unprecedented boom, demographically and economically, followed by years of retrenchment and stagnant waves. But on campus, the boom just kept booming—to the point at which enrollments broke the 20 million mark in 2009, and have remained there in the years since. And yet that continued growth in undergraduate enrollment has not been met with a commensurate investment in higher education. On the contrary. State legislatures have drastically reduced support for their colleges and universities, offloading the costs onto students and their families, redefining higher education as a private investment rather than as a public good. In the University of California system, for example, in-state tuition was $300 as late as the year 1980 (out of state, it was a whopping $360). Today, it is over $11,000. We regard this as nothing less than an intergenerational betrayal: the people whose educations were subsidized in the 1960s and 1970s, the Boomers of the boom years, graduated, became taxpayers, lobbyists, and legislators, and decided not to fund the system from which they benefited so dramatically.

It is routinely asserted that the current state of affairs, for academic jobseekers, is the result of an overproduction of PhDs. Like the claim about undergraduate enrollments in the humanities, this claim is usually presented as self-evident, and is followed with some loose talk about "supply" and "demand." And like the claim about undergraduate enrollments, it is very wrong. As Marc Bousquet has been arguing for years, the faculty workforce is made up of hundreds of thousands of people who do not have a PhD—which, we would add, effectively calls into question the function of the PhD as a credentializing degree for college teaching. (That is why the deprofessonialization of the professoriate has consequences for graduate programs.) The National Study of Postsecondary Faculty was discontinued in 2004, but as of then, 65.2 percent of non-tenure-track faculty members held the MA as their highest degree—57.3 percent in four-year institutions, 76.2 percent in two-year institutions.[16] There is no reason to think that those percentages have gone down in the past decade, and every indication that they have risen. To wit, there are many factors affecting the working conditions of adjuncts, but the production of PhDs isn't one of the major ones.

These numbers have implications that go far beyond the usual debates about the size of doctoral programs, because they illustrate how inadequate it is to think that we can solve the problem of contingent faculty simply by advocating that everyone be converted to the tenure track. Precisely because adjuncts are so invisible, even to the tenured and full-time non-tenured colleagues they work among, it is not widely understood that many of them have held their jobs—at one institution or at many, on a year-by-year basis or on multiyear contracts—for ten, 15, 20 years, and more. (Indeed, one of the most heartbreaking stories about adjuncts in the past few years involved one Margaret Mary Vojtko, who died destitute at 83, having lost her $2556-per-course adjunct job after teaching at Duquesne University for 25 years. She received no severance pay, no pension, nada. Her case is extreme, and very complicated, but notable nonetheless.[17]) Uninformed people tend, we have found, to speak of contingent faculty in two ways: either as bright, energetic 30-year-olds who enliven their departments and disciplines, working in the trenches for a few years before getting their first tenure-track job, or as professionals with day jobs in other lines of work who agree to teach a course at a local university for pin money. That part-time, informal arrangement for people who have other sources of income (be they actors, entrepreneurs, tinkers, or tailors) is the original function of adjunct faculty, and offers the only legitimate rationale for paying a college teacher less than $7000 for a college course; the Modern Language Association recommendation is for a minimum of $7230 for a standard three-credit course, and for a teaching schedule of six courses per term—for a very modest annual salary of $43,380. (Most adjuncts teach eight courses or more.)

The situation is complicated further by the terms of art by which institutions designate contingent faculty. They can be called "instructors" or "lecturers" or "visiting assistant professors" or "professors of the practice"—or pretty much anything. There is no universally agreed-upon designation for contingent faculty; there are even contingent faculty who do not want to be designated by the term "contingent faculty." By contrast, on the tenure track, an "assistant professor" almost always designates someone who has not yet earned tenure; an "associate professor" almost always designates someone who has earned tenure (in very rare cases, people have been tenured while retaining the rank of assistant—cases too rare to be important); and "full professor" almost always designates someone who has risen from the rank of associate by means of a national or international system of peer review, to promotion at the highest rank of the faculty (leaving aside further striations in rank, including "distinguished" professorships and endowed chairs; these do not come with any formal promotion in rank beyond that of full professor). And there is no correspondence between a contingent-faculty member's title and his or her rank or degree of job security. As a result, some contingent faculty are effectively long-term, full-time, non-tenure-track faculty working on multiyear contracts for decades; some are hired on an annual basis by one institution, year after year (until they are summarily let go); still others, informally known as "freeway flyers," cobble together an existence by teaching at two or more different institutions in an area—a course or two here, a course or two there. This is by far the most precarious form of academic employment, though it must be said that all contingent faculty are in a sense "precarious," and all are subject to the fluctuating employment needs of their departments—which means, in many cases, that they are not informed about what they will be teaching until mere weeks (or days) before the start of classes, or (even worse) not informed that they will not be teaching at all until mere weeks (or days) before the start of classes.

To make matters even more complicated still, while many (if not most) contingent faculty would prefer positions on the tenure track, some would not—as they repeatedly informed me during my time as MLA president. This is so for a variety of reasons. Some faculty actually teach off the tenure track voluntarily: some prefer a teaching-intensive position to a position that includes requirements for research and service, or, as one creative writer said to me, "don't you go dragooning me onto your campus committees—and I will do my creative work on my own time, thanks." Some were hired into full-time, non-tenure-track positions as part of spousal/partner arrangements in which the spouse/partner works on the tenure track. Others, including some of my non-tenure-track colleagues at Penn State, report that they chose to seek full-time positions off the tenure track because it allowed them to decide where they want to work—namely, here. (The tenure-track world, by contrast, ordinarily gives job candidates about as much control over their geographical location as military recruits have—namely, none.) There are positions among these that no doubt should be continued (with more job security) for all kinds of programmatic reasons, but if we are to reform a system most of us agree has fallen into serious disrepair, the status quo needs to be challenged. All qualified applicants should have an opportunity to apply for positions, and the majority of positions must have access to the academic freedom the tenure system makes possible. This book hopes to explain why.

More controversially, this book will attempt to explain *how*. We propose that many full-time faculty lines off the tenure track be converted to *teaching-intensive tenured positions*. The tenure process for such faculty would involve rigorous peer review, conducted by their tenured colleagues at the same institution, but would carry no expectations for research or creative activity. (We have set out the procedures for these conversions in the Appendix.) The controversial part is that not everyone now teaching as contingent, adjunct faculty would be equally eligible for conversion to the teaching-intensive tenure track. In the course of this book, we distinguish sharply between faculty (on or off the tenure track) who are hired in competitive regional or national searches and faculty (always off the tenure track) who are hired locally by means of random ad hoc procedures that are answerable to no one. Getting college faculty back on the tenure track, we believe, involves eliminating as much random, ad hoc hiring as possible, thereby diminishing the amount of faculty hiring that works as a patronage system and increasing the amount of faculty hiring that abides by nationally recognized standards of professionalism. Moreover, our proposal would give priority to faculty who have completed the doctorate, on the grounds that (a) the doctorate is the appropriate credential for tenured faculty (except in fields where the MFA is the terminal degree, as is the case with creative writers or fine and performing artists) and (b) we are currently producing cohort after cohort of new PhDs who are dumped into a system staffed by thousands of faculty who do not have PhDs. That is the structural cause of the crisis in graduate education.

As you might imagine, current graduate students, recent PhDs, and adjunct faculty members with PhDs will find a great deal to like in this plan. Full-time non-tenure-track faculty without terminal degrees, especially those who have been teaching for many years, will be far less enthusiastic. And, of course, not every institution of higher education will agree with the proposition that the terminal degree should be the necessary credential for a job; community colleges, especially, tend not to hire PhDs precisely because they associate the degree with research rather than with teaching. We have no illusions about the difficulties involved with our proposal, and no delusions that it will meet with universal acceptance by faculty or by institutions. And of course, we believe that faculty who have been teaching for many years off the tenure track, whatever their degree status, deserve the benefits of academic due process; such faculty should be given greater consideration than faculty who have been teaching off the tenure track for only a few years.

But we strongly believe that no one is facing these problems squarely. Not only has no one proposed a fix for the people-without-PhDs problem identified by Bousquet; no one has even acknowledged that the vast majority of off-track hires follow no established procedures. The result is that the profession of teaching in colleges and universities has been eroded by unprofessional hiring practices—and none of us has been eager to admit that *all of us* engage in those practices, not just overpaid central administrators. Deans do it, department heads do it, even educated PhDs do it. And as a result, there are entire departments with majority-contingent faculty who will resist our proposal because it is "elitist." But of course, if you don't believe that a profession should abide by professional hiring practices, you have nothing to complain about when your profession finds itself deprofessionalized.

And finally, there is the question of why the general public should care about any of this. If you read any online essay about contingent faculty in *Inside Higher Ed* or the *Chronicle of Higher Education*, you will quickly find, in the comment section, that (a) the higher-ed press is read avidly by people who hate professors, and (b) relatedly, there is not a great deal of sympathy out there for adjuncts making $20,000–$25,000 a year. Especially since the near-meltdown of 2008, things have been, as the phrase has it, tough all over. It is accordingly harder than most exploitatively underpaid college professors might think to tell people that many college professors are exploitatively underpaid. It's a particularly tough sell in communities already devastated by prolonged economic hardship. But it might be possible to play on the still-widespread belief that college professors are professionals, and that parents who are sending their children to college should have some expectation that professors have the professional resources— offices, phones, mailboxes, email and library access, meaningful performance reviews, protected participation in department governance—that make it possible for them to do their jobs well. It might even be possible to do this without construing students as consumers and parents as aggrieved consumer advocates demanding that they should get what they pay for. The analogy, instead, should be to the ideals and practices of professionalism: if you need an attorney, and you go to a firm that fobs you off on an associate who has to consult with you in a hallway because she doesn't have an office, would you stand for that? Is it OK that your kid is going to a college that treats its faculty that way? Or think of it in terms of what a college promises and what it practices. Is it telling students that a college degree is a pathway to the middle class, while *paying its own instructors, with postgraduate degrees, food-stamp wages?*

This line of argument seems especially necessary when one stops to consider the primary concern most people have about college—that is, its cost. College tuitions at both public and private universities have outpaced inflation for many years; at public universities, the tuition hikes are largely attributable to the decades-long withdrawal of state support for higher education, while at private universities the increases have more to do with prestige and facilities. At both public and private universities, however, there has been a dramatic expansion in the administrative and managerial ranks—and in administrative salaries. (In this, too, academe is far from alone.) Not surprisingly, student debt has soared over the past ten to 15 years. Taking on the student loan industry is the task of another book, but we hope it will suffice to say two obvious things here. The first is that the debt apologists are fond of claiming that average undergraduate debt—now over $25,000—is no more onerous than buying a car. But of course, the young graduate might still need to buy a car; and as my firstborn child, now 29, pointed out, $25,000 will get you a very nice car by the standards of the average 22-year-old. ("I could buy two Kias for $25,000," he suggested.) The second thing is that when you are saddling 22-year-olds with $25,000 in debt—and it is a special, venomous kind of debt, undischargeable even in bankruptcy proceedings—you are giving them a powerful incentive to study subjects that (seem to) promise very quick returns on investment after graduation.

The arguments about money are necessary, because few people outside academe understand that these hefty increases in tuition have actually gone hand in hand with the seismic shift away from tenure-track faculty and toward low-wage contingent faculty. But there is another critical principle at stake here, as well. We need to tell people that non-tenure-track faculty members need a measure of job security and academic freedom if they are going to be able to do their jobs *at all*. This is dicier than it may sound at first: it amounts to telling parents, students, administrators, and legislators that they have to fight for the right of professors to challenge their students intellectually, free from the fear that they will be fired the moment they say something unfamiliar or upsetting about sexuality or evolution or American history or the Middle East. This argument will surely resonate with people who understand what higher education is all about, and who are long-term supporters of PBS, NPR, or the ACLU. They are a subset of the American electorate, but they know why academic freedom is essential to an open society, and they believe in the promise of higher education. The question is whether they can be persuaded that the promise of higher education is undermined when 70 percent of the professoriate is made up of people who can be summarily fired for upsetting the wrong person.

By contrast, there is probably no way to make the case for tenure and academic freedom to people who oppose tenure on principle. The past 40 years have witnessed sustained and largely successful attacks on all forms of job security and organized labor, with the result that the union members are a tiny percentage of the American workforce and public school teachers have come under withering assault by charter-school merchants and their many allies in the media. When such people read that over 70 percent of American college teachers have no substantial job security and are being paid subsistence (or sub-subsistence) wages, their response is not "my gosh, that's terrible—higher education is one of our most important assets as a nation" but, rather, "good! Now let's get the other 30 percent." But there is a curious strain of anti-elitism on the left that plays into this logic as well. It goes something like this: *it is wrong for college teachers to claim special privileges for themselves, such as "academic freedom." College teachers are part of the workforce at large, not special snowflakes that require extra protection. There is nothing college teachers need—in material or intellectual terms—that every other worker in the world does not need.* This aspirationally egalitarian argument, we think, badly misunderstands the nature of academic freedom and the nature of college teaching; and we will address it when we talk about the role of contingent faculty in campus governance.

* * *

"It is sometimes said that society will achieve the kind of education it deserves. Heaven help us if this is so," University of Chicago President Edward Levi said in 1970.[18] Levi didn't say what such an education would look like, though it might well look like the one we have today. In 2015 higher education reflects the inequality of American society: a widening divide between the academic quality of the elite and that of the ordinary institutions, between well-compensated executive teams and an army of contingent professors, and between wealthy undergraduates and those shouldering crushing student debt. Universities under intense economic pressure, threatened with one fiscal challenge after another, seem to be inconceivably remote from the genteel world Levi sketched in 1970, a world suffused with "the magic of a disciplined process, self-generating, self-directing, and free from external constraints." This ideal of academic freedom, Levi continued, "describes a central thrust carried forward at particular times by enough scholars and enough institutions to have had a pervasive influence."[19] Our argument here is that despite the incredibly hostile conditions it now endures, this ideal is alive and well—and represents the only way to reverse the deprofessionalization of the profession. It is an ideal whose seemingly precarious life is renewed every time its extinction is predicted. The value of a university degree may be in question today; but the university's legitimating principle, the idea and the ideal of academic freedom, is not.

This book charts a path out of the curdling academic labor system and toward a world in which academic freedom serves the public good. We may not be able to convince legislatures to reinvest in higher education, but we can rebuild a faculty free from external constraints, a profession whose members need not fear termination simply because one irate student (or one irate parent, or one irate donor) lodges a complaint. We can revamp the tenure system to make it as applicable to teaching-intensive positions as it is now to those conventional jobs bundling teaching, research, and service. The university's legitimating mission—the passionate pursuit of insights and queries, free of coercion from church, state, or market—is as worthy an ideal as it was when the American Association of University

Professors was founded one hundred years ago. And in the following chapter, we'll give you some specific reasons why the humanities are central to that mission.

Notes

1. David Brooks, "The Humanist Vocation," *New York Times* 20 Jun. 2013: A23.
2. William M. Chace, "The Decline of the English Department," *American Scholar* (Autumn 2009). http://theamericanscholar.org/the-decline-of-the-english-department/
3. Mark Bauerlein, "English's Self-Inflicted Wounds," *Chronicle of Higher Education* 31 May 2013. http://chronicle.com/blogs/conversation/2013/05/31/englishs-self-inflicted-wounds/
4. MSNBC.com no longer carries that report in its online archive, but I discussed it at the time at the blog Crooked Timber. See Michael Bérubé, "Breaking News: Humanities in Decline! Film at 11," 16 Nov. 2010. http://crookedtimber.org/2010/11/16/breaking-news-humanities-in-decline-film-at-11/
5. The most egregious offenders were Alvin Kerman and John M. Ellis. See Kernan, *The Death of Literature* (New Haven: Yale University Press, 1992) and, as editor, *What's Happened to the Humanities?* (Princeton University Press, 1997); Ellis, *Literature Lost: Social Agendas and the Corruption of the Humanities* (New Haven: Yale University Press, 1997) and "Poisoning the Wells of Knowledge," *New York Times* 28 Mar. 1998.
6. Andrew Delbanco, "The Decline and Fall of Literature," *New York Review of Books* 4 Nov. 1999. http://www.nybooks.com/articles/archives/1999/nov/04/the-decline-and-fall-of- literature/
7. Frank Kermode, "The Academy vs. the Humanities," *Atlantic Monthly* Aug. 1997. http://www.theatlantic.com/past/docs/issues/97aug/academy.htm
8. Nate Silver, "As More Attend College, Majors Become More Career-Focused," *New York Times* 25 Jun. 2013. http://fivethirtyeight.blogs.nytimes.com/2013/06/25/as-more-attend-college-majors-become-more-career-focused
9. Ben Schmidt, "A Crisis in the Humanities?" *Chronicle of Higher Education* 10 Jun. 2013. http://chronicle.com/blognetwork/edgeofthewest/2013/06/10/the-humanities-crisis/
10. See *The Teaching of the Arts and Humanities at Harvard College: Mapping the Future*, p. 7. http://artsandhumanities.fas.harvard.edu/files/humanities/files/mapping_the_future_31_may_2013.pdf

11. Verlyn Klinkenborg, "The Decline and Fall of the English Major," *New York Times* 22 Jun. 2013. http://www.nytimes.com/2013/06/23/opinion/sunday/the-decline-and-fall-of-the-english-major.html?_r=0
12. Christopher Newfield, *Unmaking the Public University: The Forty-Year Assault on the Middle Class* (Cambridge, MA: Harvard University Press, 2008), p. 268.
13. Newfield, *Unmaking*, p. 270.
14. See Jennifer Ruth, "When Tenure-Track Faculty Take on the Problem of Adjunctification," *Remaking the University* 25 May 2013. http://utotherescue.blogspot.com/2013/05/when-tenure-track-faculty-take-on.html; "Why Are Faculty Complicit in Creating a Disposable Workforce?," *Remaking the University* 13 Jul. 2014. http://utotherescue.blogspot.com/2014/07/why-are-faculty-complicit-in-creating.html; and "What Can We Do Now that Adjunct Sections are Written Into Universities' Fiscal Survival Strategy?," *Remaking the University* 22 Jul. 2014. http://utotherescue.blogspot.com/ 2014/07/what-can-we-do-now-that-adjunct.html
15. Stacey Patton, "The Ph.D. Now Comes with Food Stamps," *Chronicle of Higher Education* 6 May 2012. http://chronicle.com/article/From-Graduate-School-to/131795/
16. David Laurence, "A Profile of the Non-Tenure-Track Academic Workforce," *ADE (Association of Departments of English) Bulletin* 153 (2014), pp. 6–22.
17. See Daniel Kovalik, "Death of an Adjunct," *Pittsburgh Post-Gazette* 18 Sept. 2013. http://www.post-gazette.com/opinion/Op-Ed/2013/09/18/Death-of-an-adjunct/stories/201309180224, and L. V. Anderson, "Death of a Professor," *Slate* 17 Nov. 2013. http://www.slate.com/articles/news_and_politics/education/2013/11/death_ of duquesne_adjunct_margaret_mary_vojtko_what_really_ happened_to_her.html
18. Edward H. Levi, *Point of View: Talks on Education* (University of Chicago Press, 1970), p. 170.
19. Levi, *Point of View*, p. 169.

1 Value and Values

Michael Bérubé

In February 2009, as the magnitude of the aftermath of the financial collapse of 2008 was becoming chillingly clear, the *New York Times* ran a story headlined, "In Tough Times, the Humanities Must Justify Their Worth." It remains one of my favorites in the "crisis of the humanities" genre, and I think it deserves a separate treatment here, for three reasons. One, the first quote (in paragraph five) is from Andrew Delbanco, sounding very much the way he did in 1999: "although people in humanities have always lamented the state of the field, they have never felt quite as much of a panic that their field is becoming irrelevant."[1] Two, the article includes conservative critic Arthur Kronman who, also reading from the 1990s playbook, insists that "the need for my older view of the humanities is, if anything, more urgent today," on the grounds that the humanities "are extremely well-equipped to address" what reporter Patricia Cohen calls "the greed, irresponsibility and fraud that led to the financial meltdown" (presumably this would entail mandatory seminars on Greek and Roman theories of civic virtue for all Wall Street traders). And three, the article saves the nut graf for *paragraph 17*:

> The humanities continue to thrive in elite liberal arts schools. But the divide between these private schools and others is widening. Some large state universities routinely turn away students who want to sign up for courses in the humanities, Francis C. Oakley, president emeritus and a professor of the history of ideas at Williams College, reported. At the University of Washington, for example, in recent years, as

many as one-quarter of the students found they were unable to get into a humanities course.

So it turns out that on one hand, the humanities continue to thrive in liberal arts schools. I suspect that 24 February 2009 was the slowest news day in the history of the planet, a day on which no men bit dogs and no dogs bit men. For might this not be the reason students go to liberal arts schools in the first place? Isn't this a little like publishing an exclusive report on how the sciences continue to thrive at MIT? But it's the other hand that matters here. The humanities apparently must "justify their worth" in large universities where *demand for humanities courses exceeds faculty capacity*, where students are turned away from the courses they wanted.

The really funny thing about that 2009 article, however, is that it was also published ten years earlier, and may even have quoted Andrew Delbanco. In that earlier version, the article's headline was, "In Flush Times, the Humanities Must Justify Their Worth." Because in 1999 we were in the middle of a robustly globalizing economy and a vertiginous dot com boom—who in their right mind would choose to major in humanities in times like those? And let us look more closely at the argument that a global financial crisis signals trouble for the humanities. By 2008, thanks to the financial deregulation of the 1990s and the credit default swap and subprime loan shenanigans of the 2000s, the people in the advanced financial sector of that robustly globalizing economy plunged us all into a Great Recession; now, somehow, this means that the *humanities* have to justify their worth? Surely this theme is going to be a permanent feature of the landscape in American higher education. Twenty years from now, when we are living in utopia, with 100 percent employment, with limitless clean renewable energy, with a world at peace and a children's theme park located at the symbolic (and cheerful) border of Israel and the Republic of Palestine, we will still be asking ourselves—*can the humanities be justified in times like these?*

In this chapter, I'm going to try to justify the worth of the humanities in tough and in flush times. Most of my remarks will center (justifiably, I hope) on my own discipline of literary studies—which has so often served as both the clearinghouse for interdisciplinarity in the humanities and as one of the softest targets in the academic version of the culture wars. And I'll start by citing the language of the letter I received a few years ago as part of an invitation to an event devoted to the future of the liberal arts, because I think it crystallizes just why we have found it so hard to make a compelling public case for the vital importance of the humanities:

> A traditional liberal arts education has theoretically affirmed the belief in the existence of a certain kind of knowledge or wisdom—as opposed to information, or content—that is timeless and universally valuable to the human spirit.

The dean who sent me the letter made it clear that this was emphatically *not* her own position: she was instead paraphrasing a traditional, Kronman-esque view of the humanities from which she took her distance. But I think she had it just about right: traditionally, this is very much the kind of thing we used to say. There is a certain kind of knowledge or wisdom that is timeless and universally valuable to the human spirit, and we humanists have access to it. Come take our classes, and you can have access to it as well. That was a good sales pitch: timeless, universally valuable knowledge and wisdom R us. The problem is, that dean was also right that we don't make this pitch anymore. We can't, in good conscience. We don't believe that knowledge is timeless, for one thing. And we don't believe that anything is universally valuable, either. We still believe in wisdom, I think. But you're not going to catch us saying anything about "the human spirit," because that would be homogenizing and essentializing and also mystifying, and who wants that?

Over the next few pages, I'll try to explain how things got this way. I'll breeze over the last couple of decades of literary and cultural theory, and though I will be brief I will try to be judicious. Then I'll suggest what kind of sales pitch we might want to make instead, and how we might go about justifying an enterprise that offers a form of knowledge and wisdom that is neither timeless nor universally valuable.

The shortest explanation for our aversion to talk about timelessness and universality is that We Are All Heracliteans Now. Heraclitus, for those of you who don't use the word "Heraclitean" in conversation, was the pre-Socratic gadfly who went about Ephesus telling people that everything changes except the law that everything changes, and that you cannot step in the same river twice. Over the past three or four decades, humanists are more likely to have been influenced by Barbara Herrnstein Smith on the "contingencies of value" or Fredric Jameson on the imperative to historicize, but it's more or less the same ever-changing river we're talking about: nothing is timeless or universal about human knowledge; all is timebound, contingent, partial. And the contemporary critique of timelessness and universality goes further, arguing that any attempt to represent a form of knowledge *as* timeless or universal is inevitably an ideological move, an attempt to represent a part for the whole, to claim that the intellectual folkways of one tribe are in fact models for the entire species, everywhere on the globe. It's that imperializing gesture—the very claim to universality—that makes the Enlightenment look bad in retrospect. Because it is what allowed some very bright white guys to talk about universal principles while denying that those universal principles apply to (say) women or Africans.

That critique of the Enlightenment, I believe, had to happen—for pretty much the same reason that Thurgood Marshall's critique of the Constitution as a flawed document had to happen. This is no coincidence, for the founding documents of the United States are very much products of the Enlightenment, and the Declaration of Independence's proclamation that all men are created equal cannot be reconciled with the Constitution's protection of slavery. In 1987, therefore, Justice Marshall delivered a searing speech that (predictably) drew heavy fire from conservatives for whom the bicentennial of the Constitution was supposed to be an occasion for the celebration of American exceptionalism and the wisdom of the Founding Fathers. "This is unfortunate," Marshall wrote,

> not the patriotism itself, but the tendency for the celebration to oversimplify and overlook the many other events that have been instrumental to our achievements as a nation. The focus of this celebration invites a complacent belief that the vision of those who debated and compromised in Philadelphia yielded the "more perfect Union" it is said we now enjoy.
>
> I cannot accept this invitation, for I do not believe that the meaning of the Constitution was forever "fixed" at the Philadelphia Convention. Nor do I find the wisdom, foresight, and sense of justice exhibited by the Framers particularly profound. To the contrary, the government they devised was defective from the start, requiring several amendments, a civil war, and momentous social transformation to attain the system of constitutional government, and its respect for the individual freedoms and human rights, we hold as fundamental today. When contemporary Americans cite "The Constitution," they invoke a concept that is vastly different from what the Framers barely began to construct two centuries ago.[2]

Marshall was not speaking the language of literary theory, but the broadly historicizing claim is the same: the Constitution, as a concept, is vastly different than it was when it was written. Likewise, the meaning of "human rights"—and indeed "all men are created equal"—has changed dramatically over the course of two centuries and more: "'We the People,'" Marshall wrote, "no longer enslave, but the credit does not belong to the Framers. It belongs to those who refused to acquiesce in outdated notions of 'liberty,' 'justice,' and 'equality,' and who strived to better them." One does not want to paper over the contradiction between Enlightenment universalism and actual Enlightenment practice, or to dismiss the question of how a slaveholder could write that all men are created equal and are endowed with inalienable rights by saying *well, everybody did that back then*. Far better to face the past honestly, however discomfiting that may be.

As Marshall concluded:

> We must be careful, when focusing on the events which took place in Philadelphia two centuries ago, that we not overlook the momentous events which followed, and thereby lose our proper sense of perspective. Otherwise, the odds are that for many Americans the bicentennial celebration will be little more than a blind pilgrimage to the shrine of the original document now stored in a vault in the National Archives. If we seek, instead, a sensitive understanding of the Constitution's inherent defects, and its promising evolution through 200 years of history, the celebration of the "Miracle at Philadelphia" will, in my view, be a far more meaningful and humbling experience.

The critical question, therefore—both for contemporary theory and for political practice—is whether the ideals of the Enlightenment, one of which was the belief in the universal rights of humankind, were fundamentally sound and merely needed revision over the past two centuries, or whether they were rotten root and branch, and will always lead to fatal contradictions and pernicious exclusions. Clearly, Marshall's position is far closer to the former, and as such, very much in the tradition of Western liberal progressive thought: the ideals of the Enlightenment were betrayed by the very people who formulated them, but they set us on a path that allowed for the constant reinterpretation of "liberty," "justice," and "equality." The main strands of recent theory in the humanities have tended toward the latter, seeing the tradition of Western liberal progressive thought as mostly Whiggish polyannaism that will always be blind to its own inevitable failings. And though I will endorse Marshall's version of this historical narrative in this chapter, I want to make the case as strongly as possible that work in the humanities can and must challenge that narrative's potential for complacency and self-congratulation. Scholars in the humanities would be irresponsible—they would be defaulting on a profound moral obligation—if they did not seriously entertain the possibility that the Enlightenment project is not simply a process whereby human society gradually becomes better, fairer, and more inclusive.

In order to get to that very large question, though, I need to go over some more recent history, and explain what I mean by contingency—which does not have at all the same connotations here as it does in the phrase "contingent faculty." Barbara Herrnstein Smith's *Contingencies of Value* was widely misinterpreted in the public press and in general intellectual journals when it was published in 1988. Commentators accused her of "relativism," of arguing basically that the process of evaluation (whether in aesthetics, morals, or any other realm) is completely arbitrary. Poet and critic David Lehman complained that Smith's book jettisoned two centuries of aesthetic theory—as if that were some kind of capital offense.[3] Really, only two centuries of aesthetic theory? What's the big deal? Why not take the long view about such matters? It's true, Smith's was an anti-Kantian book, but she did not argue that evaluation is arbitrary and therefore pointless; on the contrary, she argued that *evaluation is contingent and therefore inescapable.* "Contingent" is not the same thing as "arbitrary": it suggests nothing more than the uncontroversial claim that value is dependent on context. Value is not intrinsic; it is always value toward an end, for some purpose or goal.

I say this is uncontroversial, because we all know that it is part of folk wisdom: beauty is in the eye of the beholder, there is no accounting for taste, to each his own. But it does have some unsettling corollaries, including the claim that human rights are neither intrinsic nor inalienable. They too are contingent, they too will change, along with everything else we humans do. We have largely stopped talking about the great chain of being and the divine right of kings; we speak instead of the universal rights enshrined in the United Nations Declaration of 1948. But today, some of us also speak of the rights of animals, which we didn't do until relatively recently in our history, because our understanding of what a rights-bearing entity is, and what a "right" is, is also subject to the unchanging law that everything changes.

Smith's book was not the only thing that stirred the pot in what has since come to be known as the "political correctness" kerfuffle of the early 1990s. There was also Judith Butler's *Gender Trouble*, which caused all kinds of trouble, and Eve Sedgwick's *Epistemology of the Closet*, in queer theory's *annus mirabilis* of 1990. And anyone who thinks that the conservative backlash against so-called "PC" didn't have a great deal to do with what Michael Warner called "the fear of a queer planet" is fooling herself. One need only point to *New Criterion* editor Roger Kimball's insistence, in response to the 1990 MLA convention, that "homosexual themes" are not "appropriate subjects for a public scholarly discussion of literature."[4] I pointed to this at the time, and it's one of those remarks that just gets more revealing with each passing year. I could also direct your attention to *U.S. News and World Report* columnist John Leo's mockery of the "transgender dorm" and the "queer prom" at Wesleyan University—15 years later, in 2005.[5] But you get the point. These boys had *issues*.

Queer theorists had—and still have—good reason to suspect that much resistance to their work is grounded in rank homophobia. And the need to defend queer theory from rank homophobes obscured, for some years, another kind of useful trouble with the queer project—its rejection of the rhetoric of the universal. "Rejection" is perhaps too strong a word, because things weren't quite so simple, but certainly few academic humanists in the 1990s felt comfortable handling the term "universal" without first donning protective outergear. Take for example this difficult passage in Butler's "For a Careful Reading," her response to Seyla Benhabib in the collection *Feminist Contentions*:

> what one means by "the universal" will vary, and the cultural articulation of the term in its various modalities will work against precisely the trans-cultural status of the claim. This is not to say that there ought to be no reference to the universal or that it has become, for us, an impossibility. On the contrary. All this means is that there are cultural conditions for articulation which are not always the same, and the term gains its meaning for us precisely through the decidedly less-than-universal cultural conditions of its articulation. This is a paradox that any injunction to adopt a universal attitude will encounter.[6]

The reason I call this a difficult passage is that it seems almost to be wrestling with itself: on the one hand, the universal is *decidedly* not universal. To each his own universal, modulated through various cultural articulations. And yet the universal is not impossible—"on the contrary," Butler writes. What, then, is the contrary of the impossible? The merely possible? Is it that the universal has only now become possible? Or perhaps that the universal has become, for us, a necessity, even though it gains its meaning only through the less-than-universal cultural conditions of its articulation? The following paragraph clarifies matters a bit—and then muddies them further:

> It may be that in one culture a set of rights are considered to be universally endowed, and that in another those very rights mark the limit to universalizability, i.e., "if we

grant those people those rights we will be undercutting the foundations of the universal as we know it." This has become especially clear to me in the field of lesbian and gay human rights where "the universal" is a contested term, and where various cultures and various mainstream human rights groups voice doubt over whether lesbian and gay humans ought properly to be included in "the human" and whether their putative rights fit within the existing conventions governing the scope of rights considered universal.[7]

Here Butler scores a hit, a very palpable hit. She is referring not only to the homophobic fear that gay marriage will undermine the institution of marriage, but also to the sorry fact that for many years, Amnesty International did not consider crimes against gays and lesbians to be crimes against human rights in their assessments of freedom around the globe. (Though Amnesty International now emphatically considers gay rights to be human rights, thereby redefining its sense of the universal, we seem to have produced another queer paradox in the intervening years, whereby some gay and lesbian activists in the West are hesitant to condemn the persecution of gays and lesbians in Iran, for example, on the grounds that to do so would be to engage in cultural imperialism. Here, suspicion of false universals, once marshaled on behalf of gay rights, now works against the expansion of gay rights.) But what Butler is doing here is, I think, rather different from what she was doing when she insisted that the universal is always culturally articulated: in noting that "the universal" is withheld from certain groups, she is complaining, rightly, that a putative universal is *not universal enough*. What we need, then, is not a culturally contingent sense of the universal; we need a more truly universal universal.

And then Butler's argument takes yet another turn. "It may be," she writes in the next paragraph,

that the universal is only partially articulated, and that we do not yet know what form it will take. In this sense, the contingent and cultural character of the existing conventions governing the scope of universality does not deny the usefulness or importance of the term "universal." It simply means that the claim of universality has not yet received a full or final articulation and that it remains to be seen how and whether it will be articulated further.[8]

To this I can only say, *well, what did you expect*? Of course the universal may be defined differently in the future, and of course we don't know what form it will take. Indeed, the idea that the universal could ever receive a "full and final articulation" seems to me nonsensical: you have to imagine a future world in which all humans agree on the meaning of the term "universal," and we all congratulate each other on finally getting *that* settled. When you put it that way, it sounds kind of preposterous. It might even involve a children's theme park located at the symbolic (and cheerful) border of Israel and the Republic of Palestine.

But strange as it may sound, one of the leading contemporary defenders of the Enlightenment *did* put it that way. Jürgen Habermas was the *bête noire* of the academic left in the 1980s and 1990s not merely because he called Foucault and Derrida "young conservatives"[9] in the course of defending "the project of modernity" (that is, Enlightenment) but especially because he construed the "ideal speech situation" as free from domination (which is good) and oriented toward consensus (which is bad). Jean-François Lyotard's reply that consensus is "terror" was beyond hyperbolic, but surely there were and are very good reasons to object to a theory of communication that takes consensus as its a priori goal. As I noted in *What's Liberal about the Liberal Arts?*, my graduate students have all learned to reject Habermas and embrace his critics (thereby provoking the question of how they managed to achieve such a consensus), whereas my undergraduates don't see anything wrong with the idea that people should try to communicate in order to achieve reciprocal recognition and consensus. But here, the point needs to be made, on Habermas's behalf, that reciprocal recognition is not the same thing as consensus; I can understand you (or try to) without agreeing with what you say. And the point needs to be conceded, *pace* Habermas, that establishing consensus as the orientation of communication *is* coercive: it's like imagining all of culture and society as a form of jury duty, and political debate as juror deliberation. We don't get to go home until we all agree: *that* will be our full and final articulation.

There are other problems with Habermas, as well: his emphasis on reason has seemed to some critics to set emotion and affect at a discount, though one can plausibly counterargue, as Amanda Anderson has done, that there are a variety of ways to understand and achieve reciprocal recognition, not all of which rely exclusively on communicative reason.[10] But in the end, I think it is better to conceive of Enlightenment universalism as an incomplete project than to dismiss it as an illegitimate one (or to claim, as Lyotard did, that the Enlightenment leads directly to the Holocaust). And the reason I think so has everything to do with my reading of Butler's critique of universalism. That critique, as I see it, launches three ultimately incompatible claims: one, that the universal gains its meaning from decidedly less-than-universal cultural conditions of its articulation; two, that some claims to universality are partial and exclusionary, and need to be more universal; three, that the universal has not received a full and final articulation. The first two claims are in tension with one another, and the first may in fact undercut the second: that is, if you grant that the universal is always articulated as the less-than-universal, it's not clear that you can fault human rights groups for having a less than universal conception of universal rights. But it's the third claim I want to focus on now, because it suggests that *the universal can always be called to account, called into question.* Universalism in these terms appears attractive to me precisely because it announces a promise whose fulfillment can never be fully and finally achieved: it does not dictate norms (despite the widespread conflation of universalism with normative theory), it does not premise equality on sameness (with regard to race, gender, sexuality, or disability), but it does say that you can always debate whether a universalist principle is sufficiently universal.

To take a parallel example from work closer to my own, in disability studies rather than queer theory: the promise announced by universalism is what motivates Eva Kittay's disability-rights critique of the social contract tradition from John Locke to John Rawls—yet another Enlightenment project. Kittay's argument in *Love's Labor*, which is picked up and elaborated in Martha Nussbaum's *Frontiers of Justice*, is that the idea of the social contract, in which "free, equal, and independent" parties form societies for "mutual advantage" (and, in Rawls's terms, establish the principles of justice from behind a "veil of ignorance" so as not to tilt the scales to their own benefit), will always exclude people with significant intellectual disabilities, who are not free, equal, and independent and cannot offer their fellow citizens the possibility of mutual advantage. Though Rawls addresses disability in what he calls the "legislative phase" of the deliberations over justice, Kittay and Nussbaum are right to see that the exclusion of people with intellectual disabilities from the foundations of justice is intrinsic to the social-contract tradition. (As Adolph Reed, Jr. has put it in another context, this is a form of "I'll come back for you" politics.) Thus even Rawls's aspiration to a universal theory of justice, in which (for example) the Rawlsian Difference Principle permits inequalities in the distribution of goods only if those inequalities benefit the least-well-off, is weighed in disability studies' version of the scales of justice and found wanting, because its form of universalism is not universal enough.

And here's the most important point. *Only* a universalist theory is open to this kind of critique; no one can plausibly critique the theory of the divine right of kings or the great chain of being for being exclusionary or hierarchical. They're meant to be; they are impervious to egalitarian challenges. If however you advance a principle as universalist, a principle that makes that open-ended promise, you are obliged to admit all comers and take on all challenges, from anyone and everyone who believes that your claim to universalism isn't sufficiently universalist. That, finally, is why I'm ultimately with Habermas (and Thurgood Marshall) in the belief that modernity is an incomplete project. The study of disability, and the history of disability, has led me to believe that only the promise of universalism holds out the hope for an adequately capacious understanding of humans and the humanities.

* * *

Now, if I may, let me turn for a moment and say a few words about my own work in this relatively new field, and why I think it matters as a branch of the humanities.

Ten or 12 years ago, I was talking with Eva Kittay, and we were complaining to each other that philosophy had so little to say on the subject of disability—except, of course, when philosophers were finding reasons why people with intellectual disabilities do not meet their standards for entities entitled to something called human dignity. So for some years now, I've been in the position of saying to my colleagues in philosophy, "your silence with regard to cognitive disability is most dismaying," followed in short order by "actually, your undervaluation of the lives of people with cognitive disabilities is even more dismaying. I liked you all better when you were silent." Since I have an adult son with an intellectual disability, this is personal for me in various ways—but it is also a challenge for the humanities more broadly, as well. I will elaborate on one of those ways, because it will highlight nicely the difference between theories about humans that are open to endless egalitarian challenge and theories that are not.

In his 1994 book, *Rethinking Life and Death*, Peter Singer famously claimed that "to have a child with Down syndrome is to have a very different experience from having a normal child. It can still be a warm and loving experience, but we must have lowered expectations of our child's ability. We cannot expect a child with Down syndrome to play the guitar, to develop an appreciation of science fiction, to learn a foreign language, to chat with us about the latest Woody Allen movie, or to be a respectable athlete, basketballer or tennis player."[11] For those of us who work with people with Down syndrome, in whatever capacity, this is a deservedly infamous passage; and I have spent the past two decades and more watching my son Jamie rebut it all by himself. But I need to admit that back in 1994, when Jamie was only three, I might have fallen for this; I did not know what to expect when we had Jamie, but I did expect that I would have "lowered expectations" for him. What I've found, though, is that I have to keep moving the goalposts—or, more accurately, that Jamie keeps moving the goalposts for me.

Now, it's true that Jamie doesn't play the guitar; I'll give Singer that much. But Jamie's interest in *Star Wars* and *Galaxy Quest* has given him an appreciation of science fiction, just as his fascination with Harry Potter has led him to ask questions about justice and injustice, innocence and guilt. (As we were reading the final book in the series back in 2007–8, Jamie kept asking whether Harry would "turn into Voldemort" in the end. It is a very good question, as Rowling's readers well know. Since then, we have read Philip Pullman's *His Dark Materials*; Tolkien's *The Hobbit* and *Lord of the Rings*; and then, for something completely different, Fitzgerald's *The Great Gatsby*.) Jamie has learned the rudiments of a foreign language; according to the arrangement we worked out with his quite wonderful high school French teacher, he took French 2 for two years, just as he took French 1 for two years. Jamie learned some genuinely difficult things—the *passé composé* form of the past tense (*être* and *avoir* as auxiliary verbs), two forms of future tense (one using *aller* as auxiliary verb), reflexive verbs (*je me lave, tu te lave*), and then, at the very end of French 2, the imperfect tense, which

41

was a bit too much. In the meantime, Jamie has learned enough French to be able to converse with a very impressed North African man he met in the kitchen of a restaurant in Florence (don't even ask how he got into the kitchen), and to be able to charm young women at the cheese counters of French supermarkets by saying "je voudrais du chèvre, s'il vous plait." I confess that neither of us has the least interest in chatting about the latest Woody Allen movie; but this takes me to another level of argument.

Some years ago I had an exchange with Peter Singer about this passage, and part of the exchange turned on the interpretation of Singer's phrase, "we cannot expect." I had two responses. One, I do, in fact, enjoy a small handful of Woody Allen movies here and there, such as *Broadway Danny Rose* and *Bullets Over Broadway*. But there's a more important point at stake in speculating on what people with Down syndrome can and cannot understand. In the 1920s we were told that people with Down syndrome were incapable of learning to speak; in the 1970s, we knew that people with Down syndrome could speak, but we were told that people with Down syndrome were incapable of learning how to read. OK, so now that we know they can speak and read and do any number of other things, the new performance criterion for being considered fully human is suddenly the ability to chat about Woody Allen films. Twenty years from now we'll be hearing "sure, they get Woody Allen, but only his early comedies—they completely fail to appreciate the *hommages* of *Interiors* and *Stardust Memories*."

The second point is a bit broader, but follows directly from the first, and it goes to the heart of what we now call "social constructionism," which is an unfortunately loose and baggy name for the Heraclitean stress on contingency I elaborated above. For me, the merits of social constructionism, with regard to an understanding of Down syndrome, are palpable and obvious: early intervention programs have made such dramatic differences in the lives of people with Down syndrome over the past few decades that we simply do not know what the range of functioning looks like, and therefore do not rightly know what to expect. Because what has changed about Down syndrome in the last 50 years? Not the biology—not the chromosomal nondisjunction that gives people with Down syndrome an extra twenty-first chromosome. That is precisely what it has always been—a major error during meiosis. What *has* changed are the social policies and social practices through which we understand Down syndrome—and, if you will, through which we "administer" Down syndrome. That is the real challenge of being a parent of a child with Down syndrome: it's not just a matter of contesting other people's low expectations of your child, it's a matter of recalibrating your own expectations time and time again—not only for your own child, but for Down syndrome itself.

For who could have imagined, just 40 or 50 years ago, that the children we were institutionalizing and leaving to rot could in fact grow up to become actors? (I mention acting not because it's the *ne plus ultra* of human achievement but because it requires a level of self-awareness and self-fabrication that no one would have thought possible for people with Down syndrome a generation ago.) I take issue with Singer's passage, then, not because I'm a sentimental fool or because I believe that one child's surprising accomplishments and observations suffice to win the argument, but because as we learn more about Down syndrome, we honestly don't know what constitutes a "reasonable expectation" for a person with Down syndrome.

More than this, I take issue with one of Singer's central premises—one that is shared by philosopher Jeff McMahan: namely, the belief that cognitive capacity is an index of one's moral status as a being. This belief is tied strongly to—in fact, serves as the basis of—Singer and McMahan's advocacy of animal rights. Singer insists that the only secular reason humans can endow themselves with rights that they deny to animals is that we base those rights on our superior cognitive abilities (that is, those of us who do not base them on our possession of immortal souls). Mere species membership alone is insufficient, for Singer and for McMahan, as a basis for distinguishing ourselves from animals; that is "speciesism," and they regard it as analogous to racism. (It is a terrible analogy, if you stop to think for a moment about the difference between interracial sex and interspecies sex—a difference only the most troglodyte racist would seek to elide.) Indeed, Singer argues that if he is making his argument to a rational alien who understands him, he therefore has more in common with that alien than he does with a human being with significant intellectual disabilities:

> if it happens that one of you is an alien who has cleverly disguised yourself in a human shape, but you are capable of understanding this argument, I am talking to you just as I am talking to members of my own species. In important respects, I have much more in common with you than I do with someone who is of my species but, because he or she is profoundly mentally retarded, has no capacity for verbal communication with me at all.[12]

This is not funny stuff. It is, frankly, horrific. And yet the comic possibilities must be remarked. I seized upon one of them at the conference at which Singer presented this paper, and announced during the group photo that I am indeed a sentient alien in human shape, and do not see any basis for Singer's belief that he has anything important in common with me. One might also adduce Kent Brockman, the anchorman from *The Simpsons*, who, when he believes that the space shuttle has been taken over by giant space ants, famously announces, "and I for one welcome our new insect overlords! I'd like to remind them that as a trusted TV personality I could be helpful in rounding up others to toil in their underground sugar caves!" Or one might adduce the renowned "To Serve Man" episode of *Twilight Zone*, imagining a tall, smiling, telepathic alien being who is touched by Singer's refusal to eat meat on principle but cannot wait to sink his teeth into a finely prepared Singer.

As for McMahan, his moral calculus is, if anything, still more reductive—and amazingly, it is based partly on the delusional belief that we have, on balance, been too kind to people with significant intellectual disabilities, relative to animals:

> While our sense of kinship with the severely retarded moves us to treat them with great solicitude, our perception of animals as radically "other" numbs our sensitivity to them.... When one compares the relatively small number of severely retarded human beings who benefit from our solicitude with the vast number of animals who suffer at our hands, it is impossible to avoid the conclusion that the good effects of our species-based partiality are greatly outweighed by the bad.[13]

Thus, in somewhat more technical language, "the treatment of animals is governed by stronger constraints than we have traditionally supposed, while the treatment of the cognitively impaired is in some respects subject to weaker constraints than we have traditionally supposed."[14] Or in less technical language, we have undervalued the lives of some sentient animals and overvalued the lives of some humans with severe cognitive disabilities. The first of these propositions is undeniably true; the second is very close to batshit insane, at least from the perspective of anyone familiar with the history of the institutionalization of "the cognitively impaired." But such is the importance of cognitive capacity for McMahan. Indeed, he goes so far as to argue that if we devised cognitively enhanced "supra-persons," they would have a far higher moral status than we currently assign ourselves:

> suppose, for the sake of argument, that we all agree on a rough threshold for the sacrifice of an innocent person: namely, that it would be permissible to sacrifice the life of one innocent person if that were the only means of preventing

not significantly fewer than a thousand other innocent people from being wrongfully killed. Next suppose that supra-persons would not only exceed us in psychological capacity by more than we exceed the highest nonhuman animals but would also, and as a consequence, have a substantially higher capacity for well-being, both synchronic and diachronic, than we have. Finally, suppose that they would also have significantly greater average longevity. Given those assumptions, it does not seem implausible to suppose that it could be permissible to kill one innocent person as a necessary means of saving significantly fewer than a thousand supra-persons—perhaps 950, or nine hundred. Nor does it seem implausible to suppose that it would *not* be permissible to sacrifice one innocent supra-person to save a thousand ordinary innocent people. It might take the saving of eleven hundred, or even two thousand innocent people to override a supra-person's right not to be killed, or not to be sacrificed.[15]

Well, I'm glad *that's* cleared up now. I personally think 950 is too fine a calculation—we are safer in rounding to the nearest hundred. And, of course, when we are talking about the proportionate killing of innocents, so much depends on our accurate translation of that mysterious book the supra-persons gave us, "To Serve Man."

The fact that these utilitarian defenses of animal rights set many human beings at a serious discount is not a bug in their philosophical system; it's a central design feature. And it needs to be understood as such, especially by advocates of animal rights who regard Singer as an intellectual hero but clap their hands over their ears and go "la la la la la" when he starts talking about people with intellectual disabilities. And, once again, note the difference between the Singer/McMahan account of rights and a universalist account: a poststructuralist critique of universalism has some purchase on Enlightenment liberalism, precisely because the "you have systematically excluded X from

Value and Values

your understanding of rights-beating entities" can be heard and accommodated by Enlightenment universalism. By contrast, Singer and McMahan, and philosophers in that tradition, can reply to "you have systematically excluded X from your understanding of rights-bearing entities" by simply saying, "yes, thank you, that is precisely what I meant to do."

I trust that it is clear by now that disputes over the boundaries of universalism have consequences—for how we understand ourselves as humans, and for how we think about what it means to be a rights-bearing entity. But there's another aspect to the study of disability as well: I like to say that studying disability eventually entails studying everything else. One example should suffice. It's drawn from Douglas Baynton's important essay, "Disability and the Justification of Inequality in U.S. History." Baynton starts by noting that because the United States was founded on universalist and egalitarian principles, inequality is not assumed to be "natural"; rather, it needs to be justified somehow. And time and again, the principle of justification has been disability. Why can't the slaves be freed? The argument was that they lacked the cognitive abilities necessary for freedom. Similar arguments were offered for withholding the vote from women. And so women and people of African descent were placed in a most difficult position: they had to demonstrate that they were not intellectually disabled, or that equal rights would not disable them—and they often had to do so by distinguishing themselves from people with intellectual disabilities, who were rendered all the more abject and more emphatically excluded from the social contract as a result. Likewise, the story of American immigration is centrally about disability, both physical and intellectual, though it is not often told that way: the inspections at Ellis Island, which led to one-quarter of prospective immigrants being sent back to their native countries, were meant to determine—often by remarkably shoddy and capricious means—whether new arrivals were physically and cognitively capable of supporting themselves.

To put this dramatically—but accurately: you cannot understand the history of debates about citizenship in the United States without understanding the history of disability.

* * *

Now let me go back to where I began, with my remarks about the status of the humanities in American academic life. As you may have gathered in the preceding pages, there is something of a gap between the enthusiasm I feel for disability studies and interpretive theory, and the feeling of malaise and despair that suffuses so many discussions of the present state of the humanities. There is a good reason for that, and thousands of graduate students know it: this is what makes graduate study in the humanities so fraught, so full of contradiction for so many professors and students. The sheer intellectual excitement of the work, whether the work is on globalization or subjectivity or translation or sustainability or disability, is one thing. This work is so valuable, and offers such sophisticated and necessary accounts of what value is. And yet when we look at the dismal academic job market for humanists and the abusive working conditions of contingent faculty, we can't avoid the conclusion that the value of the work we do, and the way we theorize value, simply isn't valued by very many people on campus or off.

So let me be clear. I am not arguing that anything I have written here with regard to theory and universalism, the Enlightenment and its discontents, disability and social justice, has anything to do with student enrollment or institutional funding in the humanities. It's not as if students would be streaming to our courses if only we gave up all this talk about the "heterogeneity of language-games" and dwelled instead on the formal properties of the sestina and the pastoral elegy. Likewise, it's not as if taxpayers, parents, alumni and donors are sitting out there, arms folded, saying "I'm not going to support the humanities until those professors start talking about how disability should inform our understanding of universalism." On the contrary. I am arguing not that contemporary work in the humanities has driven away students, but that dire, tiresome laments *about* work in the humanities serve as self-inflicted wounds—and that some of us perversely enjoy them. I am thinking especially of the work of William Deresiewicz, who once blamed his elite education in the humanities for the fact that he could not hold a conversation with his plumber: "There he was, a short, beefy guy with a goatee and a Red Sox cap and a thick Boston accent, and I suddenly learned that I didn't have the slightest idea what to say to someone like him. So alien was his experience to me, so unguessable his values, so mysterious his very language, that I couldn't succeed in engaging him in a few minutes of small talk before he got down to work. Fourteen years of higher education and a handful of Ivy League degrees, and there I was, stiff and stupid, struck dumb by my own dumbness. 'Ivy retardation,' a friend of mine calls this."[16]

"Ivy retardation" is indeed a serious diagnosis, and might even assign one a lower moral status in the Singer/McMahan scale of moral worth; but I am beginning to suspect if some people no longer trust or respect humanists, then it is because some of us write solemn essays about how their elite educations have rendered them incapable of making small talk with plumbers. Quite seriously: if your plumber is wearing a Red Sox cap and talks with a thick Boston accent, and you can't even say a few words to him about the recent history of the Red Sox, that's not the fault of your elite education—it's just your ignorance of baseball. A year later, Deresiewicz published a review essay in *The Nation* in which he wrote,

> In literary studies in particular, the last several decades have witnessed the baleful reign of "Theory," a mash-up of Derridean deconstruction, Foucauldian social theory, Lacanian psychoanalysis and other assorted abstrusiosities, the overall tendency of which has been to cut the field off

from society at large and from the main currents of academic thought, not to mention the common reader and common sense.[17]

The claim that theory cut the field off from the main currents of academic thought is simply wrong, since of course theory was an interdisciplinary phenomenon, not only cutting across disciplines but helping to create interstitial areas of knowledge between and around disciplines; but the claim that it cut the field off from *common sense* is even stranger. It reminds me of a wonderful fantasy interview with James Dobson of Focus on the Family, published by the comic geniuses responsible for the blog known as Fafblog:

FB: I thought gay people were good and deserved marriage licenses!

JD: That's probably because of your treacherous liberal education. It's brainwashed you into thinking that there is no right and wrong, that everyone deserves equal rights, and that the fossil record accurately represents the geological and biological history of the earth. If our society continues to slide down this slippery slope of moral relativism, it will mean the end of Western Civilization.

FB: Oh no! Not Western Civilization! That's where all my friends live![18]

When I hear that literary theory has cut us off from common sense, that's exactly my reaction—Oh no! Not common sense! That's where all my friends live! More seriously, if the humanities *were* dedicated to the reiteration and reinforcement of common sense, why would they be worth a lifetime of study?[19]

It's all well and good to snark at silliness like this, but these self-inflicted wounds hide other self-inflicted wounds. In the last 15 years of the twentieth century, the public image of the humanities became most widely associated with the Paul de Man scandal and the Sokal hoax. I have always believed that the de Man affair would have had exactly zero implications for the discipline of literary criticism and theory if everyone in the discipline had responded more or less the way Barbara Johnson did: *my god, I had no idea, this is terrible*. Full stop. Because the revelation of de Man's wartime journalism for the collaborationist Belgian newspaper *Le Soir*—and I think this applies as well to more recent revelations of de Man's perfidy—tells us nothing about deconstruction as a practice of reading. However, many of the responses to the de Man affair told us a great deal about the cult of personality that had developed around certain theorists.[20] Similarly, the initial responses of Andrew Ross and Stanley Fish to the Sokal hoax took a bad situation and promptly made it immeasurably worse. I agree with David Albert that Sokal's hoax didn't actually prove that theory or poststructuralism or cultural studies was actually wrong about anything, but did reveal, in Albert's words, "something alarming about standards of scholarship in certain quarters, and standards of argument, and highlighted how much could be gained by simply declaring allegiance to certain kinds of agendas."[21] It is as if, in the 1980s and 1990s, we had a cohort of theorists whose idea of damage control was basically a form of damage enhancement. I wonder, therefore, when people attribute the decline of the humanities to the rise of interpretive theory, whether they are saying this because theory itself is a bad thing, or because what they're really objecting to is the *culture of* theory—with its superstars and shibboleths and sacred cows, its disciples and acolytes, not to mention its various forms of pledges of allegiance. Because that culture could indeed be, and often was, obnoxious.

Still, the central question remains. If indeed we no longer believe that there is a certain kind of knowledge or wisdom that is timeless and universally valuable to the human spirit, what do we tell people about the value of what we do? Is it possible to make the case for the humanities and the liberal arts without going back to the bromides of the admissions brochure? Should we simply pretend that the past 30 years of intellectual history didn't happen, or that it was all a wrong turn? Should we take a page from *The Eternal Sunshine of the Spotless Mind*, and expunge our awareness of the contingencies of value and the arbitrariness of the sign? Can we do that? Can we issue a bulletin that says from now on, words will have simple, singular, straightforward meanings, and meaning itself will henceforth be stable? Should we say that it was a mistake to develop this new field of disability studies, and that we're going to go back to the days when the disciplines of philosophy, history and literature did not address such matters? Of course not. Those cows are not going back in that barn, and I have no desire to try to herd them. Instead, I'm going to try saying that the liberal arts we now practice, the disciplines of the humanities that emphasize historical change and the contingency of value, are not only more adequate to the world we actually live in but more *exciting* intellectually: that world is a world in which the meaning and the value of Shakespeare or Sophocles or Stephen King are not fixed once and for all but open for continued discussion and contestation ... as they manifestly are. It is a world in which race and gender, sexuality and disability are not defined once and for all but susceptible to slippage and performativity ... as they manifestly are.

To put this another way: even when I disagree with sweeping denunciations of the Enlightenment and its legacy, I believe with all my heart that arguing about things like universalism is *precisely* what we're supposed to be doing. Learning and debating the history of universalist aspirations and challenges thereto, with reference to race and gender and nationality and sexuality and disability: this is what gets me out of bed in the morning. I think it is a path to a form of wisdom (yes, I still believe in wisdom, if not in timeless truths), to a deeper understanding of human affairs.

It is sometimes said that the humanities teach us how to understand "difference," in some kind of generally tolerant

Value and Values

way. I would like to believe this, because I would like to believe that when people begin to become acquainted with the history of human thought and the astonishing variety of the artifacts of the human imagination, they are more likely to see the world with a sense of wonder, with a livelier sense that any one of us might be wrong or only partly right, with an awareness that the world was not always thus and can be imagined otherwise, and with what Buddhists call "beginner's mind." But all that is merely what I like to believe. I need not puncture that belief daily by reminding myself daily that the architects of the Holocaust were intelligent and cultured men; I can temper my optimism more gently, by recalling that there is no way to ensure that training in the humanities leads to anyone's moral improvement—or even to anyone's greater happiness. As for understanding difference, we all seem to wind up, do we not, with different ways of understanding difference. But I do think, as I suggested in *What's Liberal*, that the humanities help us to grapple with the stubborn fact that some forms of difference might be unresolvable, and that some kinds of conflict might be intractable. That stubborn fact takes many shapes, from the trivial to the critical; in one of its guises, it poses to us the question of how to develop and how to maintain pluralist societies that include people who aren't pluralists. Is it right and just to exclude the excluders? Or is it arrogant and imperialist to campaign for gay rights and women's rights around the globe? What are our obligations to our descendants and our fellow species? What are the appropriate limits to genetic engineering, to prenatal screening and diagnosis? Answering those questions requires extraordinary suppleness of mind, and a willingness to think in ways that don't immediately reach for easy resolution.

An education in the humanities is not a guarantee, or a guarantor, of anything. But it may very well enhance our capacity to imagine incommensurability—and to question whether the incommensurability in question is really an incommensurability or just a dispute masking a broader underlying agreement.

And it may very well enhance our capacity to deal with real incommensurability when we see it. The question here is nothing less and nothing other than the question of how we, individually and collectively, are to lead our lives. It is a question that has vexed us for as long as we can remember, and it is a question that can only be definitively answered by our extinction, which we may yet bring about, dragging any number of species with us. But until then, we must make the case as forcefully as possible: the humanities are disciplines of lifelong learning, not providers of tasty desserts in a meal whose main courses consist of business administration and technology transfer. There are all too many people, at every university, who see the humanities as dessert—or, even worse, as a bitter pill—and it remains an open question as to whether universities will continue to be places that try to foster lifelong learning. That is why it will not suffice to see the humanities as the study of fine objects and timeless truths. We should, rather, see the humanities as the study of what it means and has meant and might yet mean to be human, in a world where "the human" itself is a variable term, its definition challenged and revised time and time again. We should say that what we offer is not the prospect of a better life but the (ancient, and ever-changing) promise of an examined life: and just as the universal has not yet received a final articulation, we might say that the study of the humanities has no final examination.

Notes

1. Patricia Cohen, "In Tough Times, the Humanities Must Justify Their Worth," *New York Times* 24 Feb. 2009. http://www.nytimes.com/2009/02/25/books/25human.html?pagewanted=all
2. Thurgood Marshall, "Remarks of Thurgood Marshall at the Annual Seminar of the San Francisco Patent and Trade Law Association," Maui, Hawaii, 6 May 1987. http://www.thurgoodmarshall.com/speeches/constitutional_speech.htm
3. David Lehman, *Signs of the Times: Deconstruction and the Fall of Paul de Man* (New York: Poseidon Press, 1991), p. 25. I discuss this

passage, and Lehman's book, in "Exigencies of Value," chapter 3 of Michael Bérubé, *Public Access: Literary Theory and American Cultural Politics* (New York: Verso, 1994).
4. Roger Kimball, "The Periphery v. the Center: The MLA in Chicago," *New Criterion* 9.6 (Feb. 1991). http://www.newcriterion.com/articles.cfm/The-periphery-vs-the-center-the-MLA-in-Chicago-5411. Kimball went on to complain that "panels devoted to homosexual themes often have the air of rallies for the initiate" but prefaced this remark by noting that "this is not because I suffer from 'homophobia.'"
5. John Leo, "Campus Life, Fully Exposed," *U.S. News and World Report,* 10 Jan. 2005. Rpt. http://wesleyanargus.com/2005/01/25/campus-life-fully-exposed/
6. Judith Butler, "For a Careful Reading," in Seyla Benhabib, Judith Butler, Drucilla Cornell, and Nancy Fraser, *Feminist Contentions: A Philosophical Exchange* (New York: Routledge, 1995), p. 129. For a brilliant reading of the Butler-Benhabib exchange, see Amanda Anderson, "Cryptonormativism and Double Gestures."
7. Butler, "For a Careful Reading," pp. 129–130.
8. Butler, "For a Careful Reading," p. 130.
9. Jürgen Habermas, "Modernity—An Incomplete Project," in Hal Foster, ed., *The Anti-Aesthetic: Essays on Postmodern Culture* (Seattle: Bay Press, 1983), p. 14.
10. Amanda Anderson, "Argument and Ethos" and "Beyond Sincerity and Authenticity: The Ethos of Proceduralism," in *The Way We Argue Now: A Study in the Cultures of Theory* (Princeton University Press, 2006), pp. 134–187.
11. Peter Singer, *Rethinking Life and Death: The Collapse of our Traditional Ethics* (New York: St. Martin's, 1994) , p. 213.
12. Peter Singer, "Speciesism and Moral Status," in Eva Feder Kittay and Licia Carlson, eds, *Cognitive Disability and its Challenge to Moral Philosophy* (Boston: Wiley-Blackwell, 2010), p. 336.
13. Jeff McMahan, *The Ethics of Killing: Problems at the Margins of Life* (Oxford University Press, 2003), pp. 221–222.
14. Jeff McMahan, "Cognitive Disability, Misfortune, and Justice," *Philosophy and Public Affairs* 25.1 (1996), p. 31.
15. Jeff McMahan, "Cognitive Disability and Cognitive Enhancement," in Eva Feder Kittay and Licia Carlson, eds, *Cognitive Disability and its Challenge to Moral Philosophy* (Boston: Wiley-Blackwell, 2010), p. 364.
16. William Deresiewicz, "The Disadvantages of an Elite Education," *American Scholar* Summer 2008. http://theamericanscholar.org/the-disadvantages-of-an-elite-education/#.U-TTQPldUqs. Regrettably, Deresiewicz has since expanded this complaint to book length, in

> *Excellent Sheep: The Miseducation of the American Elite and the Way to a Meaningful Life* (New York: Free Press, 2014).

17. William Deresiewicz, "Adaptation: On Literary Darwinism," *The Nation*, 20 May 2009. http://www.thenation.com/article/adaptation-literary-darwinism
18. Fafblog Interview Week: Fafblog Interviews Dr. James Dobson. 25 May 2004. http://fafblog.blogspot.com/2004/ 05/fafblog-interview-week-fafblog.html
19. For a comprehensive defense of theory in the context of "crisis in the humanities" discourse, see Paul Jay, *The Humanities "Crisis" and the Future of Literary Study* (New York: Palgrave Macmillan, 2014).
20. The most comprehensive array of responses to the de Man scandal is Werner Hamacher, Neil H. Hertz, and Thomas Keenan, eds, *Responses: On Paul de Man's Wartime Journalism* (Lincoln: University of Nebraska Press, 1988).
21. David Albert, John Brenkman, Elisabeth Lloyd, and *Lingua Franca*, "*Lingua Franca* Roundtable," in *The Sokal Hoax: The Sham that Shook the Academy* (Lincoln: University of Nebraska Press, 2000), p. 254. My argument that Ross and Fish made things worse is laid out in the first chapter of Michael Bérubé, *Rhetorical Occasions: Essays on Humans and the Humanities* (Chapel Hill: University of North Carolina Press, 2006).

2 Slow Death and Painful Labors

Jennifer Ruth

In the introduction, Michael suggests that this book sprouts from an email exchange in 2013. On my side, I'd start the story ten years earlier—in 2003 when I wrote Michael the first time. I asked his opinion on what I took to be signs that sparks of activism in the profession were being smothered by a theoretically sophisticated quietism.

An assistant professor at the time, I was working on the manuscript of *Novel Professions: Interested Disinterest and the Making of the Professional in the Victorian Novel* (2006), which threads present-day concerns about academic deprofessionalization into the book's arguments about the emergence of the professional class in nineteenth-century Britain. I was reading books like Michael's and Cary Nelson's *Higher Education under Fire: Politics, Economics, and the Crisis of the Humanities,* which had come out in 1995; Michael's *Employment of English: Theory, Jobs, and the Future of Literary Studies* (1998); Bill Readings's *The University in Ruins* (1996); and Stanley Aronowitz's *The Last Good Job in America* (2001). Marc Bousquet's "Waste Product of Graduate Education" essay had just been published in *Social Text* (2002). Julie Schmid, now Executive Director of the American Association of University Professors (AAUP), headed the chapter at my university—Portland State—and shared with me the galleys of *Cogs in the Classroom Factory: The Changing Identity for Academic Labor,* ed. Deborah M. Herman and Schmid (2003).

In 2003 there were plenty of reasons to believe, in other words, that the profession had achieved some clarity after a long spell of sleepy confusion. ("Don't worry," our mentors had mistakenly assured my generation; "There will be jobs when you finish your Ph.D. because a wave of retirements are predicted about then.") Now people were articulating the profession's dysfunction in explicit terms and, furthermore, recognizing that the situation stemmed not from any alleged unpopularity of the humanities but from departments' failure to hire tenure-track faculty in proportion to student enrollment. Rather than create decent jobs with the promise of academic freedom after a probationary period, somebody somewhere (everybody everywhere) was seeding a shadow workforce—badly paid, lacking benefits, shut out of university governance, stuck. Surely grasping the problem meant we were getting closer to solving it?

Yet no sooner did we collectively understand that the crisis of the humanities was a crisis of employment (not content) than we seemed to collectively decide that the socio-economic factors driving the crisis were beyond mortal control. Some people might remember this as the moment they learned David Harvey's name; some remember it as the day they found out they could use "neo" as a prefix with "liberalism." Personally, I think of it as the moment *Cultural Capital* hit. John Guillory's *Cultural Capital: The Problem of Literary Canon Formation* actually appeared in 1993 and was reissued in 1995. It was a kind of sleeper, though, that stealthily expanded its hold over critics because its basic argument, so far-reaching and so well-made, could explain more than what was really at stake in disagreements over who should and who shouldn't be included in the canon. It could explain what was really at stake in *every* development in literary studies since 1970, from the canon wars to the emergence of cultural studies to the rise of queer theory to the "pre-professionalism" of graduate students. All of these developments were, on Guillory's reading, misrecognized attempts to restore the lost cultural capital of literary study. "The cultural capital that literature used to represent has been devalued," George Levine, citing Guillory, concluded in an issue of the *ADE Bulletin*, "and we must recognize this loss.... In accepting the deflation, we have to recognize and act on the recognition that it almost certainly means that downsizing will be permanent."[1]

So in 2003 I wrote to Michael:

> I am disturbed by Guillory's analysis of the profession and by the influence that analysis is having among literary critics. The upshot of Guillory's larger-structural-changes-in-the-economy-outside-of-our-control argument is nothing short of quietism. I was glad to see you take issue [in *Employment of English*] with his starting premise about dropping enrollments as well as to see you clarify that whether literature's cultural capital has declined or not is a separate issue from whether literature remains a desirable major and vocational asset. It was worrisome, then, to read George Levine's review of your book in *Contemporary Literature*. He is clearly persuaded by Guillory and implies that you are with them on this. He puts, I think, misplaced emphasis on your line that "the market works by variables that have nothing to do with the profession's intellectual interests." I think you're right, but the way Levine takes this line as proof that you can be assimilated into the sociological quietism of Guillory is clearly wrong, on my reading.

Michael generously answered this email from a stranger at some length:

> John [Guillory] is as smart as any ten people put together. But what's happened in the shift from rabble-rousers like me and Cary to more august and austere theorists like John is that (as you point out) most commentary on the profession has now taken the tack that there's only so much we can do about our working conditions, because, after all, larger structural changes etc., so why bother unionizing, or creating

wage floors, or publicizing unethical departmental practices? After all, as Guillory has shown, the relation of cultural capital etc. Now, when John did this to the canon debate in the 1980s, it was great—he brought to that already-predictable debate a long-overdue recognition that the most important determinant of the readable is the bar of literacy, and that if we theorize the canon in relation to the emergence of the vernacular languages in Europe around 1400, then we can get a long-range perspective on the relation of education to literacy and to the canonical. I loved his essay "Canonical and Non-canonical" in *ELH* back in 1987—it was like going up to someone and saying, "does it really matter whether Zora Neale Hurston is on my syllabus?" and hearing, "well, if we go back to Dante's decision not to write in Latin...." But when he does this kind of thing with the current job crisis, it leads to some pretty mistaken conclusions, I think.

As for Levine, I think you're right. I'd meant to say that it's either foolish or disingenuous for the Ellis/Kernan crowd to claim that English has lost enrollments thanks to its trendy emphases on race-class-gender, and that the real story is that faculty lines have declined even as enrollments have risen or held steady. A fortiori, it's foolish or disingenuous to claim that the intellectual interests of faculty in English have a determining effect on the availability of jobs in the profession.

"Faculty lines have declined even as enrollments have risen or held steady," Michael wrote. This has been the real story all along. Straightforward, simple. It is cheaper for a university to hire an adjunct instructor than a tenure-track professor.

"Part-timers who have kept careful time logs," Joe Berry writes in *Reclaiming the Ivory Tower: Organizing Adjuncts to Change Higher Education,* "have reported that, when all time is counted, they often made less than $10 per hour, excluding their commute time to multiple jobs."[2] At Portland State University, a whopping

92 percent of every tuition dollar earned by an adjunct instructor is net revenue compared to 24 percent of each dollar for full-time faculty. At state institutions like mine where, according to a recent PSU publication, state support dropped over a period of two decades from 80 percent of the budget to 11 percent, the adjunct approach quickly became irresistible.

Guillory's argument muddied the waters because while he was right about the large-scale economic transformation America had been undergoing since 1970, he inferred from it some unwarranted conclusions for the liberal arts. He concluded that the humanities had lost value in the eyes of the university's constituencies—state legislators, university bureaucrats, tuition-paying parents and students—and that there was little to be done about it. My impression is that many of us were so taken with the breadth of Guillory's knowledge about the economy and with the dazzling ways he mapped socio-economic changes onto the evolution of literary studies that we only half-registered that we were simultaneously accepting the inference—the assumption that we were no longer desirable in any form and must downsize. When we thought about downsizing, though, we assumed that we would get smaller in gross numbers. We weren't thinking that the number of faculty would remain steady or even increase but that our working conditions would deteriorate. Of course, had the subpar working conditions been imposed in one fell swoop or been imposed on *all* of us, we would have understood what we were up against. But it happened over time and it happened to some of us while others of us remained comfortable. In this context, not only could people believe that our slow death was inevitable, but they could even tell themselves that the *bravest* among us were those with the intellectual chops to stare death in the face while submitting to it.

When I wrote Michael again in 2013, I brought up this earlier exchange and he laughed at the way I held *Cultural Capital* somehow accountable for how little we've done to fix the profession. He's right, of course. Within three years of finishing *Novel Professions*, I was serving as chair of my department. Now I had an up-close and personal view of the many factors that have conspired to render tenure-track faculty passive bystanders in—and unwitting accomplices to—the erosion of tenure. And shortly I will explain some of the intellectually less stimulating dynamics that make fatalism perversely attractive to too many of us. I still reserve a little place in my brain, however, where I go to grieve how a politically activist approach to the profession, so promising at the turn of the century, was drowned for more than a decade in a broad socio-economic narrative of inexorable decline. "If there is a scandal to be found in Bourdieu's sociology of art," Allen Dunn writes, obviously in another context but nonetheless summing up for me a critical disposition that has held us back, "it is in the implication that we can attain freedom only by assuming the position of spectators who witness the spectacle of human misery without being able to intervene, without being able to translate sociological knowledge into social practice."[3]

* * *

Now, of course, sociological knowledge *is* being translated into social practice. By whom? By the people who bore the brunt of the new dispensation—not the ones who thought they saw the writing on the wall and retreated to their offices, depressed but otherwise unbruised. If you've read Julie Schumacher's novel *Dear Committee Members,* you might consider the latter group to be the Jay Fitgers of the world. "We are not hiring in the liberal arts at Payne," Jay writes in one of his letters, though an aside clarifies that his department does hire but only to staff adjunct sections, "and as a result I fear we are the last remaining members of a dying profession. We who are senior and tenured are seated in the first car of a roller coaster with a broken track."[4] With little or no help from the Jay Fitgers, contingent faculty and graduate students wishing to avoid lives of precarity are slowly but surely changing the terms of our deprofessionalization.

Determined to use professional associations to combat the deprofessionalizing effects of adjunctification, activists are running for Modern Language Association (MLA) leadership positions. Graduate students in disciplines served by the MLA have organized into a force, erecting their own "Subconference" to advocate for restoring decent jobs in their disciplines. A number of national organizations mobilizing adjunct faculty across all disciplines have formed in the past five years and quickly achieved an impressive degree of visibility. The New Faculty Majority led by Maria Maisto, for example, "is dedicated to improving the quality of higher education by advancing professional equity and securing academic freedom for all adjunct and contingent faculty." The Service Employees International Union (SEIU) started Adjunct Action, "a campaign that unites adjunct professors at campuses across the country to address the crisis in higher education and the troubling trend toward a marginalized teaching faculty that endangers our profession." The American Federation of Teachers (AFT) "represents the largest number of adjunct, part-time and nontenure-track faculty—more than 100,000" and is working to organize more. All of these efforts have won legislators' attention. The US Representative George Miller (D-California) and others serving on the House Committee on Education and the Workforce submitted a report in February 2014 entitled *The Just-in-Time Professor: A Staff Report Summarizing eForum Responses on the Working Conditions of Contingent Faculty in Higher Education*. One possible outcome of this report might be the passage of the Part-Time Worker Bill of Rights Act of 2013, an act making part-time faculty eligible for Affordable Care Act coverage as well as family and medical leave protections.

There is no question that activism within the profession is now alive and well. I see the future playing out in a number of positive ways, some more positive than others if you're concerned (as we are) with better pay and benefits for all faculty and also with repairing the broken tracks of the tenure system. I want to emphasize here, though, that *none* of the potential paths forward would be possible if it weren't for this concerted and considerable effort on the part of contingent faculty. Adjunct activists and their unions are out ahead of most tenured faculty and administrators who seem paralyzed in contrast— struck dumb by magazine covers like that of the September 2014 *Atlantic Monthly*, asking *Is College Doomed?* Without the threat of part- and full-time contingent-faculty organization demanding better pay and benefits, serious reform and change is unlikely.

Before looking to the future, though, I want to explore the inertia that settled in for too long. From one perspective, it is perhaps pointless to rehearse the reasons why tenure-track faculty squandered the years after which confusion could no longer explain passivity. From another perspective, since many of us remain unskilled at connecting the dots of our own actions to the profession-wide devastation about which we read, enumerating these variables offers more than an occasion to vent.

One major reason we've been helpless to stanch the erosion of tenure is surely that we became attached to the idea of our own helplessness. We became capable of picking up the phone and calling an adjunct the day before a term begins while simultaneously believing that *we* are the hapless victims of the corporate university. An article on the Atlantic.com site quotes MLA Executive Director Rosemary Feal as saying that along with the help of trustees and accreditation agencies, the fight to reverse the deprofessionalization of humanities faculty requires the support of "middle administrators." This group "needs to choose not to be complicit in a system that abuses adjuncts," Feal said.[5] By middle administrators, I assume she has in mind the people who are central to the machinery of staffing but who nonetheless persist in seeing themselves as the corporate university's beleaguered pawns rather than its bumbling henchmen. People like Schumacher's Jay Fitger. Fitger learns at the end of *Dear Committee Members* that he is the next chair of the Department of

English at Payne University. Schumacher renders Fitger so lifelike that we cannot help but like him by the novel's close. Yet, at the same time, we know that he will do nothing to fix the broken roller-coaster track. Jay Fitger is even more of a midlife mess than Hank Devereaux Jr., Richard Russo's English department chair in *Straight Man*. Unlike Hank, Fitger won't threaten to kill a goose a day until his department receives adequate funding. He will continue, we are sure, to passively bemoan the fate of the humanities while blaming everybody around him but himself.

Why *would* he blame himself? If the dean says that there's no money for tenure lines, what is one to do? At that point, most "middle administrators" pass on the bad news and academic business proceeds as usual. He or she enlists an army of adjuncts to ensure that there are enough sections of various courses for the department's majors to graduate. Tenured faculty go ahead and launch the new minors on which they've set their hearts by hiring off-track labor. Directors of various programs continue to grow their offerings out of thin air. All of this, of course, makes life much easier for the dean, who can report more student credit hours per dollar spent. And it makes things easier for those of us on the tenure track as well.

Are we so easily bought? In all other respects, we've trained ourselves to be scrupulously ethical. Big Agro donates to the university but we publish papers tracing their pesticides to hermaphroditic fish. The state (marginally) subsidizes the professoriate but we deliver political science lectures detailing its surveillance violations. Tuition accounts for the largest portion of the state university's budget but we grade our students as if our salaries were wholly unrelated to their bills. It serves the public good for us to stand ready to bite the hand(s) that feed us. But if tenure gives us freedom from doctoring lab results for pharmaceutical donors, then it also gives us the freedom to refuse to write and sign contracts that make for widespread misery in the ranks of contingent faculty.

Refusing to create a disposable workforce (and/or a semipermanent workforce that also lacks academic freedom) would by necessity lead to solutions other than adjunctification for shrinking budgets. Surely one reason we have not forced the issue is that we are afraid that some of the solutions at which we might arrive will be unsavory—including, as they might, revising (and even increasing) workloads and/or changing the reward structures to which we're habituated. Given the enormity of the problem, though, continuing to avoid this discussion isn't an option, is it?

Nonetheless, at most places such discussions do not occur. Many chairs don't share the details of their departments' budget or its division of labor. Consequently, unless they are directors of a program, many tenure-track faculty do not consider these issues their responsibility as fellow stewards of their programs. Indeed, at too many places, tenure-track faculty remain innocent of how dependent their own departments are on adjunct labor. If you ask them how many adjuncts their department hires each term, they make a wild guess (and in my informal survey, they guess too low). In this environment, growing off the tenure track has happened almost effortlessly.

Innocence, though, is not the only or maybe even the primary problem here. Adjunct hiring has enabled us to do many things we want to do and don't want to give up doing:

(1) Hire people with higher courseloads to meet student demand without undertaking the hard work of time-intensive searches.
(2) Hire people with higher courseloads without asking whether this should prompt us to build a teaching-intensive tenure track or rethink our conventional jobs bundling teaching, research, and service.
(3) Hire spouses not as spousal hires but into non-tenure-track positions since they are easier to secure.
(4) Hire people for curricular areas we find alluring without committing to those areas in perpetuity.

(5) Grow niche programs on all-adjunct labor to boost our overall student-credit-hour numbers so that we have more capital to ask for tenure lines.
(6) Hire adjuncts to give full-time faculty course releases for research and other projects.
(7) Add new sections at the last minute when all the others fill up so that our students have the classes they need to graduate.
(8) Hire our graduate students in the hope that teaching experience will make them attractive for full-time jobs elsewhere.
(9) Continue to run the full gamut of courses during budget crunches that we hope are short-term but that invariably become long-term.

Some of these motivations are more understandable than others. All of them have made the world in which we now live.

Perhaps the most seductive rationale is the one in which we tell ourselves that short-term fixes will be repaired later. We say we'll initiate a new curricular area on contingent labor and demand tenure lines for it later. This strategy is used regularly, despite scant evidence that it works. Deans encourage the approach. When asked for tenure lines for new initiatives, they recommend that we go forward on contingent positions, prove the initiative's durability, and ask for investment in tenure lines later. Budgets then get worse, not better, so the golden time of investment rarely arrives. In the meantime, the percentage of the faculty workforce that is off track has increased.

I deployed the start-precarious-and-make-it-right-later strategy as chair and regretted it. The dean developed an interest in the visual arts and sent a note out to this effect. He was not offering tenure-line funds and it was too late in the year for a national search. I made clear to everyone—including, of course, the new hire herself when we hired her—that this was a one-year appointment that we would revisit as a department in a year. My hope, which I shared with her and everyone, was that in the next fiscal year we would convert the position to a tenure line in whatever area the department decided we needed most (film/media being a likely but not foregone choice) and that we'd conduct a national search.

We hired a talented, qualified woman a few of us happened to know in the city. I hated hiring this way when I knew that many people would want to apply for a film position in Portland, Oregon if we were conducting an open and fair search. At the time, though, I thought the overall strategy worth pursuing. It ended up, however, generating significant unhappiness in the department. The woman herself never pretended that I had given her reason to believe that she had more than a finite, one-year appointment. But since our many non-tenure-track faculty members were on fixed-term appointments (from one to three years), the idea that any full-time non-tenure-track faculty member would *not* be rehired—that renewal was not in all cases pro-forma—was threatening to them. In the minds of many department members, anybody in a full-time position, no matter the intent and method of their initial hiring, ought to be considered as permanent as any tenured faculty member. This compassionate sentiment comes out of anger at the casualizing forces of corporatization, but in practice it contributes to the growth of a non-tenure-track professoriate. It also leads to a reduction in the numbers of nationally advertised positions. Qualified people never learn about the jobs, because they have been effectively taken off the national, peer-reviewed market, and moved onto the local, ad hoc market where anything goes.

That fixed-term faculty member got a better job *before* the department made its final decision on the issue. We were able to conduct a national search for a tenure line the following year. Considering how contentious things had become within the department, I suspect she would have become a permanent off-track hire had she not secured another job. I know of plenty of cases in which non-tenure-track hires—opportunistically made to capitalize on often arbitrary developments—were made with the intention of trying to convert them to tenure lines with national searches later but which remained non-tenure-track without searches ever being conducted.

It's worth pausing here to remind ourselves of the costs we pay for this (motivated) inertia. First and foremost is the suffering of so many people who feel betrayed by careers that didn't pan out—after, in many cases, a decade of graduate training, which for many people is also a decade of living on Ramen noodles. Their services are needed because the students persist in existing, but what the instructors have cannot be called careers. I have in mind here, of course, the classic victim of adjunctification: the person who finished a PhD at great financial and emotional expense, would have been willing to go anywhere for a tenure-track job, but has been able to secure only adjunct sections. As Michael pointed out in the Introduction, this describes only a subsection of people on contingent appointments. Still, this particular variant of the suffering is the most upsetting.

There are serious costs to the institution as well. When chair, I researched the paths taken over the previous 15 years with regard to staffing by the different liberal arts departments at Portland State. While our department (English) did not have the worst record for off-track hiring (World Languages and Literature did), it was pretty bad. History, on the other hand, was pretty good. A clear majority of its student credit hours continued to be taught by tenure-line faculty. At the time, the difference was something like 65 percent compared to English's 27 percent. (Today, 58 percent of student credit hours in History are taught by tenure-line faculty and 31 percent in English.) I noticed, too, that whereas English faculty had a well-stocked grab-bag of complaints about the university, History faculty tended to complain about one thing: increases in class size. They had more tenure lines per student credit hours (hereafter SCH, with apologies for the budgetspeak) than we did. We had many more small classes than they did and many times more adjuncts.

I brought this difference between the two departments to the attention of a top administrator who took a laissez-faire approach to the information: both roads—smaller classes/many adjuncts vs. bigger classes/majority tenure-line workforce—seemed to him reasonable directions for a department to take. Three years later, after a threatened strike in which the "Walmartization" of faculty was a major rallying point and after a national survey named Portland State the seventh least-accessible faculty in the nation, he's changed his mind. "Clearly there are institutional implications of the choices made," he emailed me recently; "I agree that it clearly matters and has consequences."

Here are some of the consequences of adjunctification for university departments:

(1) There is a correlation between adjunct use and lower student retention and graduation.
(2) Being complicit with creating a casually hired workforce leads to diminished loyalty among tenure-track faculty to the student body. When one can be quickly and easily replaced by an adjunct, one begins to think about one's job in terms of everything *but* its teaching and mentoring elements.
(3) People anxious to secure employment even as an adjunct do not believe that the circumstances in which they work are fair or healthy (because they aren't), and so a substantial percentage of the faculty have at best an ambivalent relationship to the university.
(4) Casual access to adjuncts affects the morale among regular faculty who come to feel that course releases should be plentiful, and whose sense of entitlement precludes them from acknowledging how this swells the ranks of contingent faculty. (*I need a course release for x or y and why would you fight me on that when an adjunct is so cheap?*)
(5) It opens institutions up to greater liability. When problems arise, as they will within all ranks of faculty, it is harder to defend the university. It cannot be claimed in the

Slow Death and Painful Labors

university's defense that due diligence was performed when hires happen casually versus when departments undertake the extensive vetting involved in tenure-line searches.
(6) There are inevitable and growing public relations costs, which serve to further delegitimate the university as an institution.

To me, the saddest cost of the inertia that set in is that we've allowed another generation of faculty to lose trust in the public universities at which they teach, whether they are on or off the track. Further, the indefensibility of most forms of contingent labor, coupled with the dramatic new visibility of the student debt crisis, are now clearly calling into question the trust of the public at large. The idea that our public universities serve the common good is becoming a punchline rather than a point of national pride. "The Trigger Warning We Need: College is a Scam Meant to Perpetuate the 1 Percent" is the title of a recent Thomas Frank piece in *Salon*, a follow-up to his earlier, equally disheartening, "Congratulations, Class of 2014: You're Totally Screwed!" College, Frank would have us understand, is not a "mystical place of romance and achievement" but something more akin to "a cartel or a predator, only a couple of removes from a company like Enron or a pharmaceutical firm that charges sick people $1,000 per pill." Speaking to the Class of 2014, Frank says, "You borrowed and forked over enormous sums in exchange for the privilege of hearing lectures ... lectures that were then delivered by people who earned barely enough to stay alive."[6]

Frank is right: the flip side of the overextended student is the underpaid adjunct. Above these two groups, tenure-track professors with salaries and academic freedom float seemingly unscathed. We consider ourselves to be fighting the good fight—decrying student debt, condemning the exploitation of adjuncts—and yet, to the public, do we look a little like the misguided mortgage broker before the crash? Taking home middle-class pay and looking the other way while adjuncts flounder and students struggle to finish subprime degrees?

Six months ago, a friend of mine gave a reading at Powells, Portland's famous bookstore. Some of his students attended and we had dinner with them afterwards. One young woman talked about needing $1500 to pay Portland State so that she can graduate. She lives with her mom in a rented apartment. Her mom can't help her. Her mom went to Portland State 20 years ago and has yet to pay off *her* student loans. By the end of the evening, I was defending tenure to a person who can't reconcile the classes she's taken with the sticker price she can't meet or with the way her mother scrapes by despite having a degree. The young woman wasn't angry or particularly resentful. She wasn't even anti-tenure exactly. She just couldn't pretend that the university quite adds up.

If it's becoming harder to defend tenure, this is not because the promise of academic freedom upon which the tenure system makes good is any less critical to the functioning of the university now than it used to be. After serving as chair, my belief in the tenure system is stronger than ever. A few of my colleagues and I made decisions that we knew improved the program but that angered some of our other colleagues. I can't say for sure that if I understood in advance how strained departmental relations would become, I would do it over again. But I hope I would. What is tenure for if not to enable you to endure unpopularity for something bigger than yourself? I can say for sure that if we were *not* tenured, we would have had little choice but to maintain the status quo if we wanted to keep our jobs.

In order to expand our numbers of tenure lines, we essentially renegotiated the departmental division of labor. We didn't think of it in those terms at the time: we were simply racking our brains for ways to convince the dean to give us more tenure-line hires. This ended up including things like giving out fewer course releases in order to prove that we were using full-time faculty effectively. It meant that classes that had been chronically under-enrolled (at 20 with a 35 student cap) were starting to creep up to their caps because we were hiring fewer adjuncts in an attempt to avoid the trap of generating SCH cheaply for the university. ("We will grow SCH," we said, "but not through contingent appointments.") In our minds, the costs we were paying were small next to the prospect of more good jobs and fewer bad jobs in the department.

At the time I was surprised that people didn't see things the way we did. When I think back now to the fist-fights my brother and I had over whose turn it was to feed the dog or the period after our first daughter's birth when my husband and I were wrestling to make sure that the other spouse pulled precisely 50 percent of the parenting weight, I understand better what we were up against. As every sibling, spouse, department chair, union organizer, and university administrator knows, struggles over divisions of labor are rarely pretty.

The consolation we have is that it worked. By making clear that we would not continue to grow on the backs of contingent faculty, my colleagues and I got permission for two new tenure lines and an agreement to convert a fixed-term position when someone retired into a tenure-track position. Within two years, we had three new tenure lines that were not merely replacements for retiring tenure-track faculty. Further, during a period of budget cuts when replacement searches in other departments were being canceled (and the lost SCH surely made up through contingent labor), we made sure that we never lost a search. In sum, we made progress.

By the end of my term, though, we knew we couldn't do much more because the backlash was so strong. We thought we were asking people to work a little harder so that we could get more tenure lines and cohabit a department with a more equitably distributed division of labor. In time, with more tenure lines to share service duties, etc., we even anticipated (rightly or wrongly, I don't know) that the workload would be lighter than before, not heavier. To some people, though, it just looked like we'd predictably turned into your typical administrator, insisting everyone do more under conditions in which they already felt overtaxed. To our everlasting surprise, our struggle to reverse adjunctification had made it appear in some eyes that *we* were the neoliberal Man squeezing the ordinary (TT and full-time NTT) Joe. Nobody embarks on projects expecting to end up a pariah in one's own neighborhood. Yet how critical it is, and how fortunate I am, that tenure gives some of us the ability to weather people's displeasure when we are convinced something is worth fighting for.

The students deserve a faculty who can make independent judgments. Let one anecdote stand as example. A professor came to me with an interesting question while I was chair. She'd been in a meeting to discuss our major's course requirements; the issue was whether or not we counted too many film classes toward the major. Unsurprisingly, opinion was divided. At a certain point, the "yes's"—too many film courses—had convinced the majority, but one of the "no's" was stubborn. Finally, this faculty member blurted, "Look, I am not on the tenure track and all I teach is film. You reduce the film courses students take and I may be out of a job!" The professor in my office asked, "Should we be thinking about our own employment when we decide on curriculum or strictly what we believe to be in the best interests of our students?" Obviously, the latter. We're not here to ensure our own futures but to help students prepare for theirs. Tenured faculty have the ability to make disinterested decisions to this end that other faculty, through no fault of their own, simply don't. This matters in university politics. It matters a lot and it matters often.

The tenure system acknowledges human nature—namely, the fact that people usually won't act against their own interests, regardless of the larger context. It takes this into account by enabling faculty to deliberate and research and teach and grade without anxiety over the next paycheck warping the outcome of these activities. We don't have to vote on curricular matters to gratify our supervisors, we don't have to deliver lab results that satisfy pharmaceutical companies, we don't have to teach only the subjects our students find entertaining, and we don't have to please them when we submit their grades. We can follow our consciences and yet have some assurance that we will be able to feed our kids tomorrow. It's a rare gift and a necessary safeguard at one and the same time.

The downside of this, some would say, is that having trained ourselves to float above economic considerations, we are often disinclined to deal with the economic realities of our own departments, and we are often ill-equipped if we do. This is undoubtedly true, but the answer to this cannot be eliminating tenure. Tenure "is not ... a philosophical luxury universities could function just as effectively, and much more efficiently, without," Louis Menand writes: "It is the key legitimating concept of the entire enterprise."[7] It's the social contract between the university and the faculty: the university gives faculty the freedom to act with integrity, and the faculty legitimizes the university by striving to do so. The answer is to make the economics of universities part of the training we give graduate students—and to make participation in budget discussions an expectation we have of every full-time faculty member. While we're at it, we need to find ways to better encourage and reward participation in shared governance. We are not going to have the engaged professoriate we need unless we make service a truly valued component of tenure and promotion.

Those universities with the sharpest presidents, provosts, deans, chairs, and TT faculty will work towards restoring public trust by building back (or building up) their tenure-track positions. They can do this without breaking the bank by embracing teaching-intensive tenure tracks. We should labor under no illusions that such organizational change will translate directly into good will for universities. People who believe tenure should be abolished will assume that rebuilding a majority tenure-track workforce makes universities less accountable and less efficient. They will not be convinced by arguments demonstrating that in fact it will do the opposite: a teaching-intensive tenure track would entail more rigorous reviews than now take place at most institutions (strengthening accountability) and would eliminate the bureaucratic, economic, and psychological costs we incur when we repeatedly hire and rehire on fixed-term appointments (enhancing efficiency). Over time, however, having a stable workforce with higher morale and operating on ethical and sustainable lines would renew public trust in our institutions. From the faculty's point of view, the gain in academic freedom would be substantial—and this would be true even for those already tenured. The mixed workforce, as we discuss in the following chapter, creates a climate of self-censorship and wariness that affects the entire professoriate. Moving the substantial numbers of off-track faculty with higher teaching loads onto the tenure track will expand academic freedom for all faculty.

Put another way: it's not harder to defend tenure than it used to be because the concept is morally bankrupt; it's harder to defend tenure because everyone else seems to be bankrupt. When the economy was thriving, when the promises of American meritocracy were not hollow, tenured faculty could tell ourselves that we were do-gooders because we chose academia over careers that were potentially more lucrative. Now, surrounded as we are by people who are unemployed, underemployed, and one "restructuring" away from unemployment, how can we not be aware of the value of a system in which we are protected from capricious "at will" firings and layoffs? It's difficult to defend job security when everyone around you has been reduced to insecurity.

Many people, Thomas Frank included, blame the public university's economic woes not on its loss of federal and state support but on administrative bloat. The university, they explain, has increased its administrative class—both in numbers and in compensation—way out of proportion to its spending on academics. Michael discusses this in the Introduction and I agree that there is truth to this thesis, but it can't be the whole truth. For one, I wonder how much of the growth in academic professionals (rather than teaching faculty) has been necessary—legally and ethically. We have "equity and compliance" officers now, for example. We have legions of information technology support staff, counseling for careers and for mental health, and disability services (though only rarely are these sufficient to meet the accessibility needs of students with disabilities, which suggests that in some areas, we need more administration and staff rather than less). Some of the growth might be federally mandated and some may just be the unavoidable costs of due diligence for a twentieth-century institution. I'd like to see universities shrink their administrative class but I doubt this is the silver bullet.

Yes, let's regularly remind top administrators that there is something obscene about making 40, 50, 60 times what your French instructor of 15 years cobbles together out of adjunct sections. And let's publicize the fact that presidential salaries have gone through the roof over the past 20 years, even as the legions of adjuncts have swelled. Clearly, there is always (more than) enough money on campus—at the top. Knowing what I do about the inner workings of universities, though, I can't pretend that the top administrators are solely responsible for our problems. Top administrators are important players in this mess, but so are all those middle administrators—the deans, associate deans, department chairs, and the 30 percent of faculty who have tenure. Tenure makes us equals—not bosses and employees—and we share power in the university. This is, of course, what we mean by shared governance.

As Cary Nelson has argued in *No University is an Island*, the rise in research expectations has contributed to a culture in which involvement in shared governance activities are low on TT faculty's list of priorities. This is a major reason why adjunctification can sweep a university in two decades while going largely unnoticed. Universities that have maintained thriving Faculty Senates are the ones that seem to have made attempts to stem the erosion of tenure. Like Faculty Senates, undergraduate and graduate councils are important sites from which to combat deprofessionalization. Faculty can strategize to place people on the councils who will not approve new courses or programs if they are going to run on adjunct labor. Service on university-wide committees may be tedious at times, but it's almost never a waste of time since it's where shared governance happens.

It's common today for faculty—even TT faculty—to deride shared governance as a myth. Running into one another in the university's corridors, we bond by denouncing totalitarian administrators. Do we believe our own talk? I wish I could. A clear conscience is a beautiful thing. Maybe at for-profit places without tenure—places like the University of Phoenix—administrators call the tune while contingent faculty dance, but at places where tenure still provides substantial job security for a share of its faculty, that's not the case. When TT faculty talk like this, it sounds to me like we're trying to absolve ourselves of responsibility for what is assuredly a complicated and guilt-inducing predicament.

Of course there are neoliberal administrators out there who advocate explicitly for dismantling tenure and who have no interest in sharing governance with faculty. Fortunately, these remain the minority. A 2013 survey by *Inside Higher Ed* found that "70 percent of provosts at public and private four-year institutions ... agree that tenure 'remains important and viable at my institution.'" Recently, Karen Kelsky, writer of the scathingly honest blog *The Professor Is In*, was asked to give a talk to provosts on the "academic life cycle." She saw this as a golden opportunity to deliver the hard truth about the *interrupted* academic life cycle, the one that starts off with all the usual promise only to hit the eternal wall of adjuncting. "Now here's the surprise," she wrote; "the provosts seemed mostly pretty open to this message. Those who spoke in the Q and A and privately to me afterward did not dispute my argument at all. Mostly, they wanted to share initiatives on their campuses to replace adjuncts with longer-term instructors with benefits. While in an audience of 60 or so I'm sure there was a range of opinion, not always expressed, by and large the reception was amazingly non-defensive, open, and interested in change."

Kelsky concludes by saying, "The one thing I learned is that it isn't quite right to tar all 'administrators' with the same brush."[8] The move to "flexible," poorly paid labor has been for the most part one of perceived economic necessity coupled with a failure of imagination, rather than the active animosity toward tenure that some faculty believe administrators harbor in their hearts. The real issue, I think, is the dramatic heightening of the tensions between administrators and faculty that result even in the best of circumstances. If, as two scholars write in a piece analyzing the literature on shared governance, the "cultural chasm defining the work of faculty on the one hand and administrators on the other, makes cooperation in the interest of shared governance difficult at best," then the pressures placed on state institutions by the loss of state support on the one hand and the proliferation of new challenges in the form of for-profit and online universities on the other have brought this culture clash to a breaking point.[9]

What keeps most administrators up at night, I imagine, is not how to squeeze more surplus value out of adjunct labor but how to keep the university doors open. While we read Henry Giroux's *The University in Chains: Confronting the Military-Industrial-Academic Complex*, they read articles in *Harvard Business Review* with titles like "The Degree is Doomed." Or they are reading *Educause Review* articles that report: "Moody's Investors Service says that there's a mixed outlook for higher education. Tuition levels, it claims, are at a tipping point, with parents and students unwilling to pay more. Moody's analysts note that to remain viable, higher education institutions will have to introduce innovations, including 'collaborations between colleges, more centralized management, more efficient use of facilities, a reduction in the number of tenured faculty members, and the geographic and demographic expansion of course offerings.'"[10] Another mention of Moody's—this one in *The Economist*—quotes someone from the agency anticipating "a death spiral" of closures for colleges that can't compete in the new era.[11]

If professors were told for the last two decades to publish or perish, then administrators are being told today to "disrupt or die." It is misguided but hardly surprising that in this environment, administrators would grow increasingly frustrated with the power tenure gives faculty. They are looking into the abyss of an increasingly cash-strapped future while our salaries appear guaranteed, and so they feel an urgency they think we do not. As Robert Poch writes in *Academic Freedom in American Higher Education*:

> The shield of academic freedom often is raised by faculty members when they feel threatened. They use this shield to protect their rights to control the curriculum, the content of a course, and the pursuit of controversial research. Sometimes the threats are real; sometimes the shield is used to protect the faculty from accountability and the realities of fiscal constraints.[12]

Under the conditions of general austerity-hysteria created by state disinvestment and "disruptive innovation," administrators' anxiety that tenure is a "shield" being used to fend off any reform or change is running high. To defend tenure, don't we need to enter into the realities of fiscal constraints and come up with some ideas of our own?

We have to hold administrators accountable for their decisions by assertively entering into those decisions. Serving as chair taught me that we have to hold ourselves accountable, too. It is hard to keep our own colleagues' eyes on the prize—the prize being more tenure lines, fewer adjunct sections. Every day as chair of a three-tiered workforce was like navigating between Scylla and Charybdis. I didn't want to tell a full professor that I would not insist the dean give her a raise at the same moment we were exerting maximum pressure on him for new tenure lines. I didn't like turning away the lovers and friends of tenured faculty who wanted adjunct sections. (The lovers and friends of non-tenure-track faculty never asked.) I didn't want to write and sign exploitative contracts in the first place. I also didn't want to field a CV a day from people who wished to teach but for whom we had no jobs. By the time I stepped down, my unhappiness at being complicit in the machinery of disposable staffing was rivaled by the unhappiness I felt spending so much time and energy working on behalf of tenure-track colleagues who did not seem particularly interested in understanding any of this.

David Perry, Josh Boldt, and other voices in higher education have called on TT faculty to recognize our shared identity with adjunct faculty as academic labor. "Be proud of being laborers, identify with your fellow workers, and organize across the tenure–adjunct divide," writes Perry in a blog post entitled "Faculty Refuse to See Themselves as Workers. Why?"[13] Though I agree with the sentiment, I wonder if this call misunderstands the current faculty culture. Perry wants to reach those tenured faculty who mistakenly believe the hierarchy is deserved and rational—the people who are comfortable with, or even relish the prestige of, being in the top tier of a three-tiered workforce. In my experience, these faculty are a minority that gets smaller every year. Instead, TT faculty, at least at poorly funded state schools like mine, tend not to see themselves as the worthy elite but as the downtrodden. This may come as a surprise to a public traumatized by the recession. Certainly, adjunct instructors might assume that TT faculty salaries, benefits, job security, and empowerment in shared governance would preclude this group from identifying with the Joads. But no. Only very rarely do I run anymore into the stock character who thinks adjuncts are there to pick up the scraps that fall off his table. I talk regularly, however, with tenured faculty members who complain bitterly about slave-driving administrators but who do not know—and, more to the point, give every appearance of not wanting to know—how many adjuncts their own departments employ and what it pays them. Telling these faculty members they should identify as labor is telling them something they like hearing. It reinforces their sense that they are overworked and underappreciated. It also acts as a kind of Get-out-of-Jail-Free card with regard to whatever guilt they may feel about the genuinely downtrodden in their midst. In short, and at the risk of sounding cynical, we are in danger of embracing the identity of labor so that we absolve ourselves of responsibility for having poorly managed our affairs and generated our own underclass.

As I will argue at greater length next chapter, I believe we need to fight for our identities as *professionals* in order to retain (or regain) our autonomy and our empowered positions vis-à-vis administrators. I don't believe I work *for* administrators but rather *with* and, when necessary, *against* them. The flip side of this empowerment is, of course, responsibility. If we have power in how things play out, then we are also accountable for how they play out. Again, *we* make the calls to hire adjuncts. We write and sign these contracts. We propose—or don't propose—motions in the Faculty Senate to reverse the proportion of on-track to off-track faculty. On our Undergraduate and Graduate committees, we approve—or don't approve—a curriculum that will run on contingent labor.

The plight of the adjunct is the collective plight of the professoriate—and yet those of us who are TT faculty are privileged. We are in a far better position to fight for change from within our universities, and there is no question that the battle we are fighting is in some sense against administrators, if only because administrators are the ones under the most direct pressure to take economic short cuts. We have to be vigilant in exposing the kind of doublespeak and rationalizations that intense pressure so often produces. The actual economic circumstances combined with the alarmist rhetoric of business journals (*Disrupt or Die!*) can lead to some Orwellian formulations.

A June 2014 *Inside Higher Ed* article entitled "More 'Intentionality' Needed" illustrates one Orwellian turn. It covers a conference sponsored by TIAA-CREF (Teachers Insurance and Annuity Association—College Retirement Equities Fund), one in which there was no Karen Kelsky in attendance to puncture the self-serving rhetoric. Billed to administrators and higher education faculty as an opportunity to "envision faculty models of the future," it appears that the "faculty models" attendees were invited to "envision" were ones in which the tenure system plays a diminished, if not non-existent, role. The "more intentionality needed" in the title refers to more intentional hiring off the tenure track. Rather than accrue an off-track force as a groping-in-the-dark, defensive reaction to financial exigencies, the TIAA-CREF spokesperson encourages everyone to continue to employ adjuncts but to do it *intentionally,* strategically, proactively. On purpose. This bit of soft reportage by *Inside Higher Ed* gives the TIAA-CREF spokesperson the final word, as the conference itself probably did: "You do it [employ adjuncts] right," Paul Yaboski is quoted as saying, "and you're waving a trophy around."

In the bosom of such a conference, administrators freely admit that adjunct employment is "a key and permanent feature of their institutions' cost structure," in the words of SUNY vice chancellor for human resources Curtis Lloyd. That university budget officers now *count on* what was once a stop-gap measure is news to nobody. It wouldn't be news either to hear that someone had confessed this in a sheepish *what-are-you-gonna-do?* tone of voice. What's new is the idea that you might win a trophy for it and that you would wave that trophy around.

Thankfully, one conference participant experienced significant dissonance at this event. Valerie Martin Conley, chair of the department of counseling and higher education at Ohio University, is quoted as saying: "'Creeping into my head-scratching' is that 'if we take on creating policies around these individuals in these positions, it becomes much harder to ignore that we've devolved into that environment.... It sort of says it's O.K. to have them.'"[14] Professor Conley doesn't say she's "scratching her head" over the paradox that she's participating in working out policies for positions she never thought should exist in the first place. She says that this quantum reality is *creeping into* her *head-scratching*. Conley's syntax feels so honest because it reveals the unhappy movement from denial to disavowal when one begins to rationalize. Only unwelcome things *creep*, and they have to be very unwelcome to creep into our head only to be kicked back out to scratch it. She seems to be telling herself: *These positions exist. They suck (bad wages, no health benefits, invisibility in the university community). We once accepted their existence by telling ourselves that they were ad hoc, temporary, circumstantial. Now we must admit that these positions are permanently baked into our budgets. So even though we continue to believe in academic freedom and a significant degree of equality among faculty, and we know that an adjunct professoriate does not enjoy these intangible goods, we have to believe all the same that very modest improvements—like hiring with more intentionality, handing out adjunct faculty handbooks—can fix this problem.*

Adjunct faculty handbooks won't fix the problem, just as tarring all administrators with the same brush gets us nowhere. Last spring, Portland State faculty voted to authorize a strike. By the time a settlement had been reached, the union had prevented big cuts to academics. It had heavily relied, though, upon a rhetoric that demonized the very top for a rotten infrastructure that was many years in the rotting. Perhaps this was necessary to mobilize the faculty? I don't know, but I do know that many of us—those in union leadership, many members of senate, department chairs and senior faculty—had been here much longer than had either the president or provost. *We* had done as much—that is, nothing—about the quandary as they had. Caricaturing one or two people will not break down the system and rebuild it along more sustainable and ethical lines.

The reality that we all need to account for ourselves sunk in when I attended a forum held by the union in the final days of bargaining. The most dramatic testimony that night was given by someone who had been an adjunct at PSU for 13 years. He talked about the letters of recommendation he'd written over those years. Letters of recommendation—like so much else at the university—presume a stable faculty paid the kind of salary and given the kind of professional status that allows him or her to do many numbers of things without negotiating for a "wage" in return.

PSU hired this person term after term, paid him pennies, and relied upon him to write letters of recommendations for a *generation* of students. Our president had been here six years and the provost one and a half. They didn't even know this adjunct existed. Who did? The chair of the department he taught in. And if the tenure-track faculty in that department did not know he existed, they should have. The fact that this person was invisible was not one person's fault—but I will not invoke the agentless phrase "broken system" here. Real people wrote these contracts; real departments relied upon this labor. We can stop. The Appendix offers nuts-and-bolts advice for reform; the next chapter explains why tenure is an essential ingredient of that reform.

Notes

1. George Levine, "Putting the 'Literature' Back into Literature Departments," *ADE Bulletin* 113 (1996), p. 14.
2. Joe Berry, *Reclaiming the Ivory Tower: Organizing Adjuncts to Change Higher Education* (New York: Monthly Review Press, 2005), p. 7.
3. Allen Dunn, "Who Needs a Sociology of the Aesthetic? Freedom and Value in Bourdieu's *Rules of Art*," *boundary 2* 25.1 (1998), p. 90.
4. Julie Schumacher, *Dear Committee Members* (New York: Doubleday, 2014), p. 105.
5. Rosemary Feal, quoted in Elizabeth Segran, "The Adjunct Revolt: How Poor Professors Are Fighting Back," *The Atlantic* 28 Apr. 2014. http://www.theatlantic.com/business/archive/2014/04/the-adjunct-professor-crisis/361336/2/
6. Thomas Frank, "Congratulations, Class of 2014: You're Totally Screwed," *Salon* 18 May 2014. http://www.salon.com/2014/05/18/congratulations_class_of_2014_youre_totally_ screwed/

7. Louis Menand, ed., *The Future of Academic Freedom* (University of Chicago Press, 1996), p. 4.
8. Karen Kelsky, "Adjuncts, Assistant Professors, and a Broken Faculty Life Cycle," *The Professor Is In* (blog), 25 Jul. 2014. http://theprofessorisin.com/2014/07/25/adjuncts-assistant-professors-and-a-broken-faculty-life-cycle/
9. Marietta Del Favero and Nathaniel Bray, "The Faculty-Administrator Relationship: Partners in Prospective Governance?" *Scholar-Practitioner Quarterly* 3.1 (2005), p. 62.
10. George L. Mehaffy, "Challenge and Change," *Educause Review Online* 5 Sept. 2012. http://www.educause.edu/ero/article/challenge-and-change
11. "The Digital Degree," *The Economist* 28 Jun. 2104. http://www.economist.com/news/briefing/21605899-staid-higher-education-business-about-experience-welcome-earthquake-digital. The Moody's official quoted is Susan Fitzgerald.
12. Robert Poch, *Academic Freedom in American Higher Education: Rights, Responsibilities, and Limitations* (San Francisco: Jossey-Bass, 1993), p. xv.
13. David Perry, "Faculty Refuse to See Themselves as Workers. Why?," *Chronicle of Higher Education,* Vitae *blog*, 22 May 2104. https://chroniclevitae.com/news/509-faculty-refuse-to-see-themselves-as-workers-why
14. Colleen Flaherty, "More 'Intentionality' Needed," *Inside Higher Ed* 23 Jun. 2014. https://www.insidehighered.com/news/2014/06/23/discussion-focuses-envisioning-faculty-models-future

3 From Professionalism to Patronage

Jennifer Ruth and Michael Bérubé

In this chapter, I tell a story about differential teaching loads and foreclosed paths to promotion, followed by an analysis of why academic freedom is indispensable for any faculty member who wants to participate in university governance. The story goes some way toward explaining why we must insist on a teaching-intensive tenure track—and the analysis, I hope, finishes the job. Too many people have either given up on restoring a majority tenure-line professoriate or don't think that academic freedom is central to the issues raised by hiring off the tenure track. Understandably, those commentators have decided that we need to focus on improving salaries and ensuring benefits. But we argue that the tenure component is essential for a couple of reasons: faculty need the protections of tenure to participate actively in shared governance, and relatedly, when faculty without academic freedom participate in governance, it tends to accelerate the erosion of tenure. So in the course of this chapter, I will be doing something at once wonky-detailed and ambitious. I hope to explain, even to people who don't know how academic hiring processes work, why hiring legions of faculty off the tenure track leads to the creation of fiefdoms and patronage systems; and I hope to show that academic freedom matters not only in research and teaching but in the grainy details of how departments and colleges are run.

In order to do all that, though, I'll need to start by explaining how elusive a concept academic freedom can be. "People differ on whether or not academic freedom resides in an individual or in the collective body of scholars (for instance in defining curriculum or scholarly acceptability), on whether academic freedom is rooted in professional standards of truth-seeking or extends to expressive speech," Michael Meranze writes. "But whatever these differences, they all presume a community of scholars with the authority and independence to determine institutional goals without fear of discipline. It is this last situation that no longer exists."[1] It no longer exists because today "the majority of faculty work in subprofessional conditions," as a 2009 AAUP document on *Tenure and Teaching-Intensive Appointments* states.[2] They are "at will" employees without the due process guaranteed to tenured faculty members. Two things follow from this. In the case of the most precarious contingent faculty members—the adjuncts hired on a course-by-course, term-by-term basis—you wind up with a cohort of faculty who have no long-term stake in the institution, because they are not *permitted* to have a long-term stake in the institution. And in the case of permanent, full-time non-tenure-track faculty, you wind up with a cohort of faculty who may owe their hiring or their continued employment to whoever happens to be the department head.

The tenure process, by contrast, follows a rigorous process of peer review that embeds faculty members within self-governing and self-regulating research and teaching communities. Fewer of our faculty members undergo such a process and earn tenure. Instead, as the AAUP report on *Tenure and Teaching-Intensive Appointments* explains, the new majority of "arrangements commonly involve minimal professional peer scrutiny in hiring, evaluation, and promotion." All faculty are affected by this sea change, including those with tenure-track appointments. When "most teachers in higher education have neither tenure nor the prospect of ever getting it," Joe Berry writes, "administrators and trustees have won a great victory ... [and] the faculty as a whole is less able to set the terms of its own work."[3]

Mary Burgan observes that "once the members of this network [of faculty] are considered to be disposable by means other than the serious judgments of peers within their fields, the trust embedded in its procedures must wither."[4] In environments in which off-track professors outnumber on-track ones, shared governance disappears. At my institution, where we have 605 tenure-track faculty, 246 full-time non-tenure-track faculty, and 719 adjuncts, the perceived deterioration of shared governance was one of the main things faculty cited when they voted to authorize a strike in 2014.

There is a way to fix this. When one track emphasizes teaching and service and another one entails teaching, research, and service, the two tracks can deliberate collectively in relative harmony—*if* individuals on both tracks have equal access to the independence achieved after passing through the eye-of-the-needle process known as tenure. When there are two tiers and one enjoys academic freedom after a probationary period while the other doesn't, they cannot. The playing field is simply too uneven to act as the foundation for genuinely *shared* governance. In order to provide the independence necessary to avoid the corruption and cronyism patronage systems invariably produce, we need to build at our institutions a system for teaching-intensive faculty that mirrors as closely as possible the tenure system that exists today for those faculty whose jobs bundle teaching, research, and service.

* * *

We recognize that shared governance among relative equals is rarely a walk in the park. There is an old joke about academia: *the fights are so vicious because the stakes are so low*. I've always wondered about this joke, since it seems to me people in all careers walk away with their battle scars. If there really is something particularly nasty about academic infighting, is it less because the stakes are low (they don't seem low to us) than because the setup is uniquely ambiguous, uniquely *horizontal*? TT faculty do not argue with one another from positions within a hierarchy (supervisor, assistant manager, etc.) but from a place of structural equality. It is notoriously hard for peers to negotiate their collective labor, and yet the conviction that professors must be peers is historically what has given the American university its unparalleled credibility. American (as opposed to, say, Chinese) universities are not intended to abide by one set of politics. They are meant to be places where people think and act independently and collaborate from a standpoint of independence. When you ask people to negotiate their collective labor, *and then* you throw people who are not vested as peers into the deliberative mix, an already complex situation can become intractable.

My story starts from the commonplace observation that the professoriate at the typical state university has been reconstituted into a three-tiered faculty of tenure-track (TT), full-time non-tenure-track (NTT), and adjunct instructors. But as John Cross and Edie Goldenberg write, we remain "remarkably uninformed about the consequences for faculty makeup, faculty priorities, academic freedom, and faculty governance of hiring large numbers of teaching and research specialists who are not eligible for tenure."[5]

"I could sue," the faculty member I'll call Mary said to me when I was her department chair. Mary is known for indefatigable niceness and a strong aversion to conflict. There is nothing less likely than that she would sue Portland State. This lent her comment all the more weight. "I *wouldn't*," she followed up quickly. She *could*, though. Mary is off the tenure track, and she has a higher courseload than her peers—though at the same salary. Just because we both knew she wouldn't sue didn't mean this irrationality didn't bother her or pose a problem for the department. Like other unexplained inconsistencies that fray morale, this one acted as a subterranean tension in a department that had grown its faculty off the tenure track for three decades. We had done so in the dark, so to speak—that is, as a makeshift approach during tenure-track-hiring freezes and budget cuts. Over time, "fast-tracked" hiring had become a habit whenever needs (and desires) arose. And they arose year after year after year.

Portland State is on the quarter system rather than the semester system; Mary teaches three courses a quarter in the English department. Faculty on the tenure track teach two courses a quarter. In our college, these teaching assignments are standard policy. TT jobs carry research and service expectations, which is why they usually require faculty to teach fewer courses. The general idea is that when all forms of faculty labor are tallied, most professors wind up working about 50–55 hours per week. As it happened, however, two of our ten NTT faculty did not teach 3/3/3 but rather 2/2/2—the same as TT faculty but with no equivalent in service or research expectations to explain the discrepancy.

This arrangement—same courseload, fewer expectations—must have seemed reasonable when a chair first offered the anomalous contracts. At that time, off-track faculty made a fraction of what tenure-track faculty made. Who could argue with reducing to 2/2/2 the load of a person making not much more than half a TT Assistant Professor's salary? But things were not so simple as that. Before I had become chair, but after those two professors received their 2/2/2 assignments, the union passed equity-at-rank salary minimums. In the English department, this meant that full-time faculty made the same salary whether off or on the tenure track. (By and large TT faculty in the English department make the minimum at rank, though a handful of TT faculty negotiated higher salaries when hired.) So now we had a situation in which two people, hired without departmental participation or review, had tenure-track courseloads and salaries but little expectation of research and service and, of course, no requirement to undergo the rigorous peer-review process for tenure.

The two faculty members given lighter teaching assignments than other off-track hires had earned terminal degrees in their field. This is almost certainly why they'd been singled out in the first place: when the inequity among assignments came up, people would mention the terminal degree as the salient variable, but this consideration was not stated in any of our governance documents, nor was it ever discussed at departmental or committee meetings. Adding to the incoherence was the fact that we regularly hire people for sabbatical replacements who have terminal degrees as well—but we give them 3/3/3 teaching assignments.

Mary, for her part, had a terminal degree. She'd earned it in a low-residency MFA program while working for us. Her rank changed from Senior Instructor to Assistant Professor and her salary increased. All well and good—but what about her 3/3/3 courseload? Was I—or the department's budget—prepared to reduce all NTT faculty loads for those who earned terminal degrees, regardless of whether that had been relevant in their hire? How would we make up the lost courses if we reduced these loads—hire yet more adjuncts? And how did any of this make sense? We hired some people in national searches, evaluating their research agendas and later determining whether or not they stay at the university based, in part, on that research. Why were we hiring some people ad hoc—without departmental review or participation and without rigorous evaluations—at the same salary and teaching load? Was there a rationale behind what appeared to be historical accident?

The dilemma illuminated so much that was wrong with our department—and English departments across the country. In 1975, we had no contingent faculty whatsoever. In 2009 (when I was chair), we had 26 TT faculty, ten NTT faculty, and more than 25 adjuncts. We had departmental policies and procedures for hiring and evaluating TT faculty, but no procedures or policies for the others. As a result, we had a workforce designed as much by who knew whom when, and by the emergencies that arose from year to year, as by professional, deliberative discussion and open nationwide searches. It became harder and harder to avoid acknowledging—if only in private conversation—that we had created a patronage system through ad hoc hiring. We had spawned a kind of new old boy network, in which some people would invariably back others in departmental decision-making for the very good reason that they owed their jobs to them. This is a common, widely recognized problem when it affects the civil service sector. Entire departments of municipal administration are overtaken by Tammany Hall-style cronyism and corruption. The fig leaf of "meritocracy" is cast aside, and what you have is naked patronage. But what most people don't realize is that a kinder, gentler version of the patronage system has been slowly institutionalized in academe with off-track hiring.

Let me step back a moment and explain why this matters. In *The Future of Academic Freedom*, Louis Menand writes, "Coercion is natural; freedom is artificial."[6] The tenure system is an artificial construction. The hiring process is baroquely elaborate, involving layers upon layers of review and deliberation, but that's what keeps it from being a system based on patronage. By the time you get your job and then achieve tenure—after interviewing, after having many people read your work and references, after visiting a campus and giving a job talk and meeting with dozens of potential future colleagues, after undergoing evaluations by committees and external reviewers—you feel legitimate. No, scratch that—you *are* legitimate, in the sense that you have gone through a legitimating process, a system designed to *legitimate* professionals as professionals, akin to bar and licensing exams but involving many more face-to-face meetings and anxious meals with search committee members.

Even when you recognize that chance always plays a big role in the academic job search (and it does), you nonetheless don't feel you owe your luck to any particular person, because ordinary academic hiring, on the tenure track, in a nationally advertised search, cannot be determined or controlled by any particular person. That's often not the case when hiring off the tenure track. When we hire off the tenure track, we create complex networks of obligation; we create potential fiefdoms. At the very least, we make our world more vulnerable to corruption: I protect your job security, you vote for me. I give your spouse a non-tenure-track position, you feel indebted to me. Hiring on the tenure track has its opportunities for patronage, of course, but it is very difficult to submit the entire process to one person's whims and desires. There are more steps, more bureaucracy, more people involved at every stage. And in this sense, if this sense only, "more bureaucracy" is a *good* thing: it is an artifact of rationalized and routinized procedures that minimize—if they cannot entirely eliminate—the element of caprice. As a result, the kind of direct-unmediated power of boss–employee is diffused in a way that it isn't with off-track hiring.

It didn't take very long to realize that a transparent, equitable policy for non-tenure-track faculty hiring and courseloads was way overdue. I understood that developing one would open a Pandora's box filled with many cans of worms, but I didn't feel like I had much choice. A department needs rational, clearly articulated reasons for practices as important as differing courseloads; otherwise, it becomes a place where faculty members are disaffected and disgruntled, and for good reasons (as opposed to reasons involving outsized academic egos and complaints about parking). Of course, the political difficulty of making formerly invisible arrangements visible is that anyone who benefits from those arrangements will feel threatened. In institutional terms, it was a job that desperately needed to be done, in the interests of professionalism and basic fairness; but in personal terms, it was a no-win situation. I recognized it as such at the time but knew that the problem would continue to fester until addressed formally. In fact, that very year, we'd hired someone for a tenure-track job who had a partner for whom she wanted us to create a non-tenure-track position. Why didn't the department do for them what it had done for another tenure-track faculty member and his spouse? We no longer had any reliable sense of what constituted "equitable" treatment for our department members. Once departmental discussion is bypassed and a special situation is created for one person, how do you justify not reproducing it for the others who come along?

There is another old joke about academia, this one about the slowness of decision-making. It takes many forms, but generally goes something like this: *suddenly, a fire broke out. Thinking quickly, the physics department convened a committee to study it and issue a report.* So I know how this is going to sound—but it is crucial to my argument that academic decision-making (in the absence of fires), like most forms of professional regulation and review, is done more reliably by committees than by fiefdoms. I convened an Ad Hoc Committee on NTT Faculty Policy. I asked two tenured faculty members and two NTT faculty members to serve on it. From the start I knew that I was putting the two NTT faculty members in a vulnerable position; I also knew that most people in my department didn't understand this. Not yet. We are a department in which full-time faculty off the tenure track are voting members, and so NTT faculty would expect to be represented in the deliberations. Creating a committee to work on NTT faculty issues and *not* putting NTT faculty on it would have been both counterintuitive and explosive.

The Ad Hoc Committee quickly realized that the situation was worse than I thought. We had unexplained inequities, that much we knew already—but we also found that we had no way of promoting NTT teaching-intensive faculty. Our own procedures did not allow for it, most likely because we had never collectively come to terms with the fact that we had a large cohort of NTT teaching-intensive faculty in the first place. The department's policies and procedures documents stipulated that if full-time faculty are to be considered for promotion, then their research record should be part of their review. But we had been hiring NTT faculty at 3/3/3 assignments precisely because we did not expect or require them to do research. We had created teaching-intensive positions, but we were effectively denying the faculty in them a path to promotion.

I anticipated that as part of its charge, the Ad Hoc Committee would rewrite the policies and procedures so that teaching-intensive faculty could be promoted on the basis of their teaching. This wasn't what they did. Instead, they decided that all university faculty should be granted time to do a little research in their careers at some point. How else, they asked, do we distinguish the college professor from the high school teacher? (This question obviously pertains to our adjunct instructors as well, but for some reason that may be attributable to our structural blindness to that third tier of academic labor, that question did not come up.) Once this point of view was accepted, the problem with the situation on the ground was not the inexplicably inequitable teaching assignments; rather, the problem was that people had unequal access to promotion. We had issued contracts with 2/2/2 teaching assignments that enabled some people to prepare themselves to go up for promotion, while others carried courseloads that made promotion impossible. The committee recommended that full-time NTT faculty have the opportunity to apply to the Curriculum Committee for releases for research. It sounded right; it sounded equitable. And in a sense, if you didn't consider the larger structural questions for the department and the profession, it was.

The recommendation made its way to the Curriculum Committee, where someone asked the question the Ad Hoc Committee had conveniently punted: how would we determine the number of course releases we could offer each year? The Great Recession of 2008–9 had sent the college into panic mode. It wasn't the ideal time to lobby hard for tenure lines (when has it been a good time in the past 30 years?) but that's what we were doing. As discussed in the last chapter, we were resisting the trend of delivering student credit hours cheaply through contingent hiring. Despite the college's mounting budget crisis, the strategy was paying off. If we asked for more course releases for NTT faculty who had been hired ad hoc, I knew the dean would stop working with us to create new tenure lines. Again, why go through the professional rigmarole of the advertised national search and the tenure-track process if we could simply hire people off track and give them course releases for research as well?

Under these circumstances, the Curriculum Committee made the best decision we believed possible. We decided to pool the existing releases from six courses per year—those already given to two of the faculty—so that all NTT faculty might apply for them. Each year, two NTT faculty would get a lower teaching assignment that would (we hoped) enable them to pursue research, but each year those releases would go to two different NTT faculty members. This seemed the only reasonably fair thing to do. After presenting this proposal to the Executive Committee, which endorsed it, I presented the recommendation to the department.

Well, you can imagine what happened next: what seemed reasonably fair to us understandably did not seem fair to the two people who'd long had lighter teaching assignments. One of these two non-tenure-track faculty members was the spouse of a tenured professor in the department, a well-regarded professor who might very well become department chair after my term ended. For obvious, understandable, and lamentable reasons, the two NTT faculty members serving on the Ad Hoc Committee did not want to risk alienating him. They were upset with how the discussions had evolved and no longer wanted to be implicated in any aspect of the recommendation. Since they would be among those applying for the releases, they concluded they had a conflict of interest—and that I should never have asked them to participate in the first place. I agreed. It was very clear now, as it hadn't been before, that it was wrong to ask faculty without tenure—that is, without the academic freedom that allows one to weigh in on contentious administrative issues without fear of reprisals—to participate in such deliberations *precisely when it affects them*, as it so often does.

As with any departmental implosion, there must be any number of versions of this story. For my part, although I have replayed the sequence of events many times, I can't find an exit to an outcome that would have been fair to everyone involved and would have put the department on a wiser path. There *is* something that I would do differently today, however. How, I wonder, would the situation have played out had I asked the NTT faculty member married to the tenured professor to serve on the Ad Hoc Committee? Had she served, might she have had to confront the same double binds we were confronting and is it possible that she would have come to similar conclusions?

The department never voted on the proposal. The whole issue became too incendiary to touch. I stepped down as chair; not long thereafter, the tenured husband became chair, just as everyone had anticipated. The couple left for another institution two years later. We still don't have an equitable, transparent policy regarding NTT faculty hiring and teaching assignments.

* * *

When contingent faculty participate in academic decision-making with tenure-track faculty, they do so on an uneven playing field—and sometimes they are thrown off the playing field altogether. In 2013, for instance (just to take one instance among countless instances), adjunct activists Keith Hoeller and Kathryn Re filed a complaint with the Northwest Commission on Colleges and Universities with regard to the capricious treatment to which they had been subjected by their employer, Green River Community College. As reported by the *Chronicle of Higher Education*,

> [t]he letter of complaint against Green River Community College ... accuses that institution of failing to protect

Mr. Hoeller and other part-time instructors from retaliation when they have been at odds with the full-time faculty members who dominate their faculty union and, as department heads, control their teaching assignments.

"Given the precarious position that adjuncts have with no job security, it goes without saying that an adjunct who says something that the tenured faculty does not like is very likely to have no classes the next quarter," it says.[7]

Indeed, when contingent faculty call themselves the serfs, peasants, or helots of academe, they drive home a real point—that their initial and then continued existence at an institution is contingent on the pleasure of individuals with tenure, even when they are represented by a faculty union. The tenured professoriate is uncomfortable acknowledging it, but the power differential warps the discussion in ways that cannot be finessed by appeals to departmental "equity" or "workplace democracy." In 2013, at a meeting of the California state conference of the AAUP, I raised this issue with an audience comprised mostly of NTT faculty members. A few of them told me that they made a point of speaking out on their campuses. I asked if they considered themselves unusual and they said yes—they were the exceptions. We agreed that the circumstances of participating in governance as NTT faculty tend to lead either to a kind of determined, exhausting outspokenness or to a defensive, self-protective reserve—neither of which of course is ideal for anyone in a workplace, let alone workers who should have every reason to expect that they can rely on professional conditions of employment.

Furthermore, as I mentioned earlier, NTT involvement in governance can accelerate the erosion of tenure. Here's how it has done so in my department:

(1) NTT involvement has made it virtually impossible to handle budget cuts in any way other than by canceling job

searches that were replacements for retiring tenure-line faculty. Who would choose to not rehire someone with whom you have been involved in all kinds of departmental and university discussions and deliberations? So when a budget "crisis" erupts (which happens every year at my university, typically *after* we've received approval to replace retired tenured faculty but *before* we've begun a search), we cancel a search. It is much easier to cut a position to be held by some hypothetical future colleague than to cut a position held by someone you see on a regular basis. Over time, this means fewer tenure lines and more NTT lines.

(2) NTT involvement creates various conflicts of interest, as it did in my department. Even discussing what areas in which to hire after someone has retired becomes complicated when an NTT faculty member has begun filling in by teaching this or that related subject. She may not have a terminal degree or expertise in the area but she, and the people who worry about her, may feel that her job will become more insecure if we hire people in certain areas. This often is not stated explicitly but instead implicitly shapes the contours of deliberation.

(3) Once NTT faculty participate in service/governance, one must ask whether it's fair for people to spend time on tasks for which they are not paid or for which their teaching assignments do not give them adequate time. We typically address this by reducing courseloads. In turn, we hire more adjuncts to replace full-time NTT faculty in the classroom. This accelerates the out-of-whack proportions—fewer tenure lines, more NTT and adjunct appointments.

(4) When NTT faculty are voting members of a department and when chairs are elected, this creates a particularly vulnerable bloc that is likely to vote for chairs who protect job security and/or are sympathetic to reduced loads. However anybody might feel about this (whether that's a good or bad thing), the outcome is a department with leadership that finds it exceedingly difficult to make reversing the

trend of adjunctification by increasing good jobs a high priority for the department.

But if NTT involvement in departmental decision-making only exacerbates the problems we've created with an off-track workforce, what is the alternative? Shouldn't every faculty member in a department have a say in how things run?

Advocates of contingent faculty involvement in governance often invoke "democracy" or "citizenship." Such language highlights the central problem with the growth in non-tenure-track faculty—what do you do about shared governance when the majority of your faculty are contingent? Are you prepared to deny whole swaths of people who teach for the university a voice in its affairs? But terms like "democracy" also make it difficult to see the underlying problems with involvement. The situation in most universities today is that only a minority of faculty are in a structurally equal position to participate in governance. "It is misleading," Larry Gerber writes, "to base the faculty claim to a primary role in academic governance on strictly democratic principles." It is not, he explains, "the principle of equal representation for all citizens, or 'one person, one vote,' that justifies the faculty's role in university governance."[8] What legitimates the professor's involvement in governance is her or his inclusion in a professional community.

The rights of the professor, in other words, are the rights of the professional who has become part of a self-regulating group. In 1915, Arthur Lovejoy and Edwin Seligman published the seminal "Declaration on Academic Freedom and Academic Tenure." They argued that the only credible authority over the professoriate is its own self-governing members:

> The distinctive and important function [of professors] ... is to deal at first hand, after prolonged and specialized technical training, with the sources of knowledge; and to impart the results of their own and of their fellow-specialists'

investigations and reflection, both to students and the general public, without fear or favor.... The proper fulfillment of the work of the professoriate requires that our universities shall be so free that no fair-minded person shall find any excuse for even a suspicion that the utterances of university teachers are shaped or restricted by the judgment, not of professional scholars, but of inexpert and possibly not wholly disinterested persons outside their ranks.[9]

The American Association of University Professors (AAUP) was formed the same year, and over the ensuing decades, the organization built a strong environment in higher education for academic freedom by developing the tenure system. The "Statement of Principles on Academic Freedom and Tenure" issued in 1940 became the gold standard for all serious colleges and universities, and to this day, the "Recommended Institutional Regulations on Academic Freedom and Tenure" make up the backbone of faculty handbooks throughout the United States.

The 1915 "Declaration of Principles on Academic Freedom and Academic Tenure" is not quite a world-historical document on the order of the Declaration of the Rights of Man and Citizen, but it did make the world-renowned twentieth-century American university possible. It did so by creating a professional cohort of university teachers whose intellectual independence gave the university its legitimacy. These teachers could not be summarily fired for running afoul of the financial or political interests of donors, trustees, legislators, or pundits. Yet, just as Hannah Arendt famously described the French declaration of rights, the rights declared by Lovejoy and Seligman are perplexing. The French Revolution document yokes "man" and "citizen" ("the rights of man and citizen"), Arendt pointed out, as if the two words are equal and even interchangeable when in reality the former depended on the latter. Once large numbers of people were rendered stateless by Europe's mid-century catastrophes, it became obvious that "man" was nobody—at least nobody anybody else had to be accountable to or for—without citizenship. Similarly, the professor's declaration of independence yokes "Academic Freedom" and "Academic Tenure" as if they, too, are equivalent or even interchangeable, when in reality the former depends on the latter. "The professor" is nobody—at least nobody anybody else has to be accountable to or for—without tenure. He/she is an at-whim employee, hired casually and simply not renewed.

Widespread reliance on contingent faculty has shattered the illusion that academic freedom exists independently of academic tenure. Faculty at some universities hope that the creation of an "Instructor Bill of Rights" will extend academic freedom to all faculty, regardless of how they are hired or reviewed. But, to borrow again from Arendt's wording in *Origins of Totalitarianism,* is there any paradox of contemporary university politics filled with a more poignant irony than the discrepancy between (a) the efforts of well-meaning idealists who insist on the universal right of academic freedom and (b) the precarious situation of the rightless adjuncts themselves? Documents like an "Instructor Bill of Rights" do not go to the source of the problem—which is that economics and expediency have driven us to erect a second and third tier of faculty without the protocols and protections of tenure. They apply a Band-Aid, a superficial remedy that will offer no substantial protection to contingent faculty when push comes to shove. From the contingent faculty member's perspective, these declarations can add insult to injury, carrying as they do a whiff of *noblesse oblige*. Equality, if it is to be real, must be institutionally produced and guaranteed, not graciously declared.

Such documents respond to the unhappy cultural and social dimensions of the contingent faculty member's predicament but do little to change the material reality—that casual hiring also means casual firing. Could it be otherwise? Can we bypass the work involved in bringing someone into a profession and then credibly claim for them the status of a member with all of a member's rights and prerogatives? No amount of good will or good intentions can preserve the professoriate's unity when it is fragmented along three ranks, only one of which is eligible for tenure. Full-time non-tenure-track faculty are as convinced as adjuncts that the loss of eligibility for tenure is identical with the loss of academic freedom. Rather than being vested members of the academy engaged in a common intellectual and pedagogical enterprise, the majority of faculty are treated as, and so rightly identify as, labor. Since the individual ladder climbed by the aspiring professional has been kicked out from under them, they place their hopes in the collective power of numbers rather than in professional *fortuna*. Since they consider shared governance a farce at the corporate university (because, for them, it is) and since the efforts of the comparatively powerful amount to little more than patronizing words like "value" and "respect," they—and other groups of faculty as well—reasonably conclude that only collective bargaining can improve their conditions. The tenure system comes to seem increasingly irrelevant in no small part because it is hard to affect the tenure system through bargaining.

How has academic freedom—the freedom from economic and political pressure that liberates disinterested judgment—become so disentangled from its material reality in the tenure system?

"We can scarcely recall that the ideal of academic freedom was formulated [in 1915] precisely to transform basic American understandings of the employment relationship between faculty and their university or college," writes law professor Robert Post. He continues:

> This amnesia is unfortunate, for it has facilitated the rise of an entirely different conception of academic freedom. In the past half-century, America has developed a culture of rights, and we have accordingly come to conceive of the structure

of academic freedom in terms of "rights of free expression, freedom of inquiry, freedom of association, and freedom of publication." We now tend to conceptualize academic freedom on the model of individual First Amendment rights possessed by all "citizens in a free society." The difficulty is that this reconceptualization of academic freedom can neither explain the basic structure of faculty obligations and responsibilities within the universities, nor provide an especially trenchant defense of the distinctive freedoms necessary for the scholarly profession.[10]

The First Amendment is a weak foundation for academic freedom since it cannot explain how the professor's academic freedom is in any way *academic*—that is, it cannot explain how the freedom of the professor in the academy differs in any way from the freedom of the citizen in the public sphere.

Post's answer is much the same as ours: the professor's academic freedom is a *professional* freedom. Unlike freedom of speech, Post writes, "rights of academic freedom are instead designed to facilitate the professional self-regulation of the professoriate, so that academic freedom safeguards interests that are constituted by the perspective and horizon of the corporate body of the faculty."[11] Post replaces the opinionated citizen-professor with the competent professional-professor working within a community of peers. It might seem that we are giving something up when we embrace the professional version of academic freedom over one that attempts to derive authority from simple citizenship. And perhaps we are. Certainly, the professional version requires us to consider the group as important as the individual. The professional *group* is the self-regulating organism, not the individual, leaving us subject to the power of our peers. There is another way to think about this, though—one that perhaps makes the professional professor as palatable as the citizen-professor.

As individual professors we are not unique and exceptional, but our employment circumstances *are* fairly unique in the modern world. Chapter 2 argued that shared governance is not always tedious. The rarely acknowledged truth is that in contexts in which everyone feels that their equality has been institutionally guaranteed, it can be profoundly rewarding. Testing one's ideas among people who are neither one's boss nor one's employees is to enjoy an experience rare in many workplaces. The freedom generated by the tenure system is the freedom to act in concert with others, to develop something together not because someone is ordering you to but because you are embarked on a common project. Academic committee work may be easily ridiculed as a professorial version of *Dilbert,* but it actually consists of professors articulating and negotiating the terms of their employment, their expertise, their research projects, their course assignments, and their engagements with students. What results from these negotiations cannot be chalked up to hierarchy; it is the outcome of genuinely shared governance. "Shared," here, does not mean that the negotiations are without heat and conflict, of course. What it does mean is that nobody has recourse to an outside authority other than reality (think budgets not bosses) to resolve the conflicts that arise. This lends the discussions their (sometimes) exhilarating air of spontaneity and authenticity.

The 1940 AAUP statement on academic freedom and tenure is formulated solely in terms of research, teaching, and so-called "extramural utterances"—covering instances in which professors "speak or write as citizens." There is no mention of these circumstances we just described, that third set of professional activities professors regularly perform (governance and service). We can say in hindsight that this oversight at the moment of conception is a significant flaw. Because AAUP focused on research and teaching and not on the political work internal to the university (governance and service), academic freedom could come to seem like something akin to an intellectual property rather than a structural feature of the modern university. A largely "negative" version—in Isaiah Berlin's sense—of academic freedom was etched and, as the decades rolled on, set in stone. As a result, Gerber notes, even though "faculties began to play a more prominent role in college and university governance in the interwar years, the principle of academic freedom and the recognition of tenure as a means of protecting that freedom won more rapid and widespread acceptance than did the notion of faculty responsibility for academic decision making."[12] It was not until May 1994 that the AAUP issued its policy statement "On the Relationship of Faculty Governance to Academic Freedom."[13]

Participation in governance requires academic freedom. We need professors to be able to exercise independent judgment collectively, as difficult as this sometimes is, when they perform the workaday business of the university, whether this involves curricular matters or discussions of MOOCs in the Faculty Senate. Why does this matter to people who don't know what a provost is, or who don't use the word "decanal" in conversation? Oddly enough, the answer was provided by the US Supreme Court in 2006, in a case that originally had nothing to do with academic administration and faculty decision-making—the case of Garcetti v. Ceballos, decided 5–4 along the Court's deep conservative/liberal divide. In 2009, as chair of the Committee on Academic Freedom and Professional Rights and Responsibilities, Michael drafted the MLA's response to *Garcetti*, which drew on the *amicus* brief filed by the AAUP and the AAUP campaign, "Protecting an Independent Faculty Voice." In *Garcetti*, Michael wrote,

> the Supreme Court held that public employees have no First Amendment protection for statements they make in the course of their professional duties. The case concerned a deputy district attorney, Richard Ceballos, who objected to misstatements made in an affidavit for a search warrant. Ceballos brought his concerns to his supervisors; when they decided to proceed with the case anyway, he spoke to the defense

attorneys in the case, and defense counsel subpoenaed him to testify. In response, his supervisors in the district attorney's office retaliated against him, denying him a promotion and transferring him to a distant location. Ceballos sued, losing in district court but prevailing on appeal to the Ninth Circuit Court. The case then went to the Supreme Court, which reversed the findings of the Ninth Circuit, concluding that public employees are not protected when they speak "pursuant to their official duties."

Even though Garcetti v. Ceballos did not involve university personnel, the Supreme Court's holding has curious and unsettling implications for academic freedom. In dissent, Justice David Souter wrote, "This ostensible domain beyond the pale of the First Amendment is spacious enough to include even the teaching of a public university professor, and I have to hope that today's majority does not mean to imperil First Amendment protection of academic freedom in public colleges and universities, whose teachers necessarily speak and write 'pursuant to official duties.'" However, Justice Anthony Kennedy's majority opinion pointedly refused to answer Souter's question, noting, "There is some argument that expression related to academic scholarship or classroom instruction implicates additional constitutional interests that are not fully accounted for by this Court's customary employee-speech jurisprudence. We need not, and for that reason do not, decide whether the analysis we conduct today would apply in the same manner to a case involving speech related to scholarship or teaching."

That is where matters stand today, except that numerous lower courts have begun to apply *Garcetti* to professors at public universities, ruling that faculty members have no protection from retaliation when they speak in the course of their official duties—which most often means "when they speak as committee members performing service work that contribute to the maintenance of the university." Perversely, the Supreme Court held that public employees can be protected by the First Amendment if their statements have no credibility whatsoever, following the precedent of Pickering v. Board of Education (1968). As Michael's MLA statement phrased it, "faculty members whose statements are utterly ill-considered and misinformed enjoy First Amendment protection from administrative retaliation, but faculty members who know what they're talking about speak up at their peril."[14]

This heightened uncertainty, coupled with the deprofessionalization that ad hoc hiring amounts to, poisons cultures of shared governance. In a predominantly tenure-track context, by contrast, the freedom one experiences among one's peers was never far from the reality when participating in shared governance. This version just didn't achieve distinct articulation. Was this because at the time the ideal was developed—the 1930s and 1940s—an emphasis on a community defined by equality might have raised the specter of communism and provoked political resistance? More likely, this alternative understanding of academic freedom went unrealized because we moderns have a hard time conceiving of freedom as necessarily plural and collective rather than defensively singular and individual. Whereas a professional version of academic freedom might have emphasized the necessity of building and maintaining a politically guaranteed and horizontal space for its exercise, the negative version of academic freedom emphasizes the autonomy of individuals. These individuals are more likely to interfere with one another than to be the condition of one another's freedom. It's as if once we realized that we needed the professor to have autonomy from overt agents of power (the board, the state, the market), we began to believe, if only half-consciously, that he should have autonomy from everybody—even his peers. Rather, as sociologist Craig Calhoun writes, professors "should be seen as obligated to carry out their work in a sufficiently public way for it to be judged by the relevant professional community."[15]

From 1940 on, a negative version of academic freedom (freedom *from*) dominated the academy, and the internal organization of faculty deliberation was typically neglected. Negative freedom prepares a mind for "idle curiosity," in Thorstein Veblen's memorable phrase from *The Higher Learning in America*. Today tenured professors avoid this phrase for good reason—the idea of idleness does not market well in this market—but we still take the point: we can't know in advance what discoveries or concepts will yield value for society, and so knowledge must be an end in itself. But "idle curiosity" is clearly the experience of the (singular) person thinking, someone in friendly conversation with him or herself. One imagines a person alone—or, rather, someone in that state Socrates calls "the two in one" that every human being becomes when he or she is thinking. "Idle curiosity" does not lead us to visualize a plurality. We don't picture the Faculty Senate debating the promises and perils of online technology or the Third Estate pounding out the Tennis Court Oath at the start of the French Revolution.

We can no longer think about academic freedom in only or even primarily individual terms, because the three-tiered faculty workforce has changed the once-horizontal space of governance into an uncomfortably hierarchical one. The nature of the *space* of governance has changed. When the professoriate engaged in governance and service was overwhelmingly tenured or tenure-track, it did not spend a lot of time worrying about internal conflicts of interest and the subtle or not-so-subtle pull of hierarchy. Senior faculty and junior faculty were aware, of course, of the power differential between them. But the idea that someone deliberating on the English major might be unable to cover his or her cost of living the following year if the committee decided to eliminate the popular culture or the pre-1800 literature requirement—this had not occurred often enough to register, not even in the retrenchment years of the early 1970s.

We haven't taken into account that the structural transformation of the professoriate entailed a massive loss of academic freedom. "For 75 percent of instructors in higher education, it is meaningless to claim that they possess academic freedom in its traditional understanding," writes Michael Meranze. And yet documents like an "Instructor Bill of Rights" suggest that we cling to the idea that the professoriate remains horizontal. The fact has not sufficiently sunk in that, as Meranze puts it, "the legal and practical underpinnings of academic freedom are weaker than they have been in decades" because the tenure system itself is weaker than it's been in decades in the sense that it applies to fewer and fewer of us.[16]

Here's a dramatic piece of evidence that the profession is in denial about the structural transformation it has undergone. In 2013, the AAUP issued a report entitled *The Inclusion in Governance of Faculty Members Holding Contingent Appointments*. The perspective of the report is ostensibly that of the non-tenure-track faculty member—and that is what makes it problematic. (This is, in fact, the report that led me to write to Michael.) "As AAUP has documented time and again," the report begins, "the proportion of faculty appointments that are 'contingent'—lacking the benefits and protections of tenure and a planned long-term relationship with an institution—has increased dramatically over the past few decades and continues to increase."[17] The report recommends inclusion of non-tenure-track faculty in most areas of governance—though it acknowledges that serious problems can arise, the greatest one being real or perceived retaliation. Can off-track professors really speak their minds when participating in governance activities alongside people with the authority to fire them on a whim?

The report does not consider that the space of academic deliberation itself is transformed when it is no longer horizontal. It is no longer an arena in which one assumes the effort of persuasion and the risk of failure among one's peers. Rather, it is an arena of the overprivileged and the underprivileged, those with job security (or the prospect of it) and those without. Above all, it is divided between people who are now, or might later be, in a position to write and sign contracts— and people whose degree of job security will depend entirely on those contracts. When the space of deliberation changes, everything about the faculty dynamic changes. The tenure-track faculty member becomes no less self-consciously aware of her power than the non-tenure-track faculty member is humiliatingly aware of his vulnerability. Spontaneity and candor are destroyed and different concerns move to the fore. The orientation of the room shifts almost palpably from a focus on the needs of the students, the institution, or the discipline to a focus on the needs of the faculty themselves. What if, to take last chapter's example, someone on the Curriculum Committee is a contingent faculty member hired to teach film classes and the agenda for the day's meeting is whether the number of film classes students use toward the English major should be restricted? In such a case, faculty are not arranged around a table but rather around an elephant in the room—the elephant being the stubborn fact that one person at the table could lose her job if the discussion goes one direction rather than another.

The AAUP report understands very well that faculty are not free from coercion when non-tenure-track faculty are involved in governance—not because it is aware of this fragile organized space, but because the report is principally concerned (as it must be) with the vulnerability of the NTT faculty member. The report only very briefly acknowledges that contingent-faculty involvement in governance introduces persons into group deliberations whose lack of job security makes it difficult, if not humanly impossible, for them to be impartial: "contingent faculty are not protected by tenure and so may be ... more susceptible to pressure from administrators or other faculty than are tenure-track faculty." Even if a given faculty member happens to be an exceptionally disinterested thinker, that won't prevent the others at the table from wondering whether the person's vulnerability affected his reasoning. Upton Sinclair once remarked that it is difficult to get a man to understand something when his salary depends on his not understanding it. It doesn't require bad blood between people for such a question to arise.

The AAUP's 1915 statement on academic freedom held that "no fair-minded person shall find any excuse for even a suspicion that the utterances of university teachers are shaped or restricted by the judgment ... of not wholly disinterested persons." With the introduction to governance of contingent faculty serving on easily evaporated appointments, a fair-minded person does have reason to wonder whether interests might warp the outcomes of group deliberations. Understandably human interests (of self-preservation), to be sure, but interests nonetheless.

It makes sense that the report's biggest concern with NTT faculty inclusion in governance is protection of the individual faculty member, not protection of the hard-won space of equality constructed for governance. After all, it is the NTT faculty member who is the victim of the deprofessionalization of the professoriate. Why wouldn't we want to compensate for that injustice by privileging her perspective? And it is appropriate, even for those fortunate enough to have tenure, to identify with our deprofessionalized doppelgangers. This is because if we are honest with ourselves, we know very well that we could have found ourselves in their places. It is also because we genuinely recoil from the idea of a faculty member whose seat at the table can be so easily pulled out from under her. "Despite the seriousness of these considerations, the solution is not to bar some faculty from service but to better protect the academic freedom of those serving in governance roles," the report concludes. It calls for institutions to address the concerns raised by their inclusion by developing policies to protect non-tenure-track faculty from retaliation. It does not indicate what such policies might look like or whether they would be enforceable without meaningful job security.

The obstinate reality is that the embedding of faculty members within stable and sustainable self-governing and self-regulating research and teaching communities happens through the work of becoming tenured—one's own work as well as the efforts of others and the resources of the institution itself. The process matters because the process, not the individuals as such, performs the work of legitimation. A vertical ladder—the tenure track—creates peers who, when together, occupy a horizontal space. Cribbing again from Arendt's discussion of the stateless in *Origins of Totalitarianism*, we can say that shared governance rests on the assumption that we can produce equality through organization, because people can act in, change and build a common world together with their equals and only with their equals. And, in turn, as Cary Nelson writes, "academic freedom is an empty concept, or at least an effectively diminished one, if the faculty does not control its enforcement through shared governance."[18]

The horizontal space of the tenured is an unusual space within a society in which most employers are reluctant to relinquish control over their employees. "The radical nature of academic freedom cannot now be grasped," Post writes, quoting Arthur Lovejoy, "unless we first recover an appreciation of how academic freedom would seem peculiar chiefly in that the teacher is in his economic status a salaried employee, and that the freedom claimed for him implies a denial of the right of those who provide or administer the funds from which he is paid."[19] The AAUP spent decades building a system that can produce this professionally useful freedom. Like all human systems that seek to replace coercion with freedom, the tenure system is not perfect; but it goes a long way toward satisfying both the needs of the faculty (both individual and as a body) and the needs of an institution that cedes power when it grants a high degree of job security.

How is the right of all faculty to academic freedom enforceable when asserted as a natural right but not bound up with a rational, rigorous, and professional process of conferring and guaranteeing that right? "The principle of academic freedom is a paradoxical one, [because] it asserts that those who buy a certain service may not ... prescribe the nature of the service to be rendered," Dewey wrote.[20] The tenure system institutionalizes this particular and paradoxical kind of freedom. It is exceptionally difficult, if not impossible, to see how academic freedom is possible without it. The AAUP report on NTT and governance wants to convince campuses to include contingent faculty in service and governance, but it can't resolve the problems it raises with such inclusion. Simple policy statements asserting that everyone involved in governance on or off the tenure track has academic freedom are not sufficient. If they were, all those AAUP committees of years past would not have felt it necessary to build the tenure system—a system of protracted professionalization beyond the credential. Clearly, we are no less vulnerable to economic pressures today than we were in 1915 or 1940; the adjunctification of the professoriate is itself the most telling sign of the university's profound economic vulnerability.

The AAUP report on NTT inclusion in governance ends not by ringing the note of freedom or of equality (both of which have proven complicated and tricky) but by invoking the term that is assumed to combine both: democracy. In the last line of the document, the word "democracy" appears for the first time: "democracy and active voluntarism must be combined with a culture of faculty solidarity across all ranks and classifications." It is hard to resist the obvious good will of an organization that functions as a democracy while simultaneously enjoying solidarity. But is this a plausible characterization of a world that can exist among haves and have-nots with regard to job security? "Although many non-tenure-track faculty have begun (with the support of the AAUP) to lay claim to a role in institutional governance," Larry Gerber writes, "their lack of job security, frequent part time status, and the fact that many part-time faculty work at more than one institution to earn a living, makes such participation problematic."[21]

"Problematic" is an understatement. With the erosion of the professionalism once institutionalized by the tenure system, the university community has not blossomed into a vibrant democracy but reverted to the kind of demeaning and resentful culture typical of patronage systems. It has devolved into precisely that "free for all" Louis Menand refers to when he says that "any internal account of what goes on in the academic world must at the same time be a convincing rationale for maintaining the space defined by academic freedom. The alternative is a political free-for-all, in which decisions about curricula, funding, employment, classroom practice, and scholarly merit are arrived at through a process of negotiation among competing interests."[22] And that is the brutal reality that no well-meaning bill of rights or AAUP statement can credibly avoid: when your department has a majority-contingent workforce, all of whom have a vote but none of whom have the protections of tenure, what appears at first blush to be "democracy" is in fact a prescription for academic neo-feudalism—and a sure way to accelerate deprofessionalization.

Professors earn their autonomy from state and market interference, and their right to deliberations free from coercion, through the self-policing mechanisms of professionalization. Only if professors hire and evaluate one another in accordance with the rigorous hiring and meaningful reviews assumed by the tenure system can they protect their autonomy and, in turn, the freedom their resulting equality makes possible for each other in governance. Because of this, Bruce Robbins acknowledges that professionalism can always be accused of being undemocratic: "professionalism is very easy to present—indeed it is hard *not* to present—as an offense against democracy. To repose interpretive authority in a community of professionals is to put it where it is not accessible to everyone."[23] Similarly, Joan Scott reminds us that "the principle of academic freedom was not, as critics sometimes describe it, an endorsement of the idea that in the university anything goes. The call for faculty autonomy rested on the guarantee of quality provided by disciplinary bodies whose role is to establish and implement norms and standards and so to certify their members' professional competence."[24]

In a manifestly inequitable workplace, the principle of broad inclusion is obviously a more appealing rallying point than the professionalizing hoop-jumping of the tenure system. Everybody is for democracy, and meritorious competition smacks of neoliberal fantasy. But "inclusion" is a just and humane sentiment rather than a sustainable system, and the AAUP report only scratches the surface of the problem we created when we let ourselves become a three-tiered faculty workforce. The equality of tenured peers is not the universal equality that is humanity's ever-moving goalpost and that is, as Michael so poignantly illustrated in Chapter 1, the proper pursuit of the humanities. Rather, it is the circumscribed equality of an academic community that selects its members and publicly recognizes their right of equality through the steps of the department-and-discipline-driven (not supervisor-driven) tenure system. By contrast, "the ways in which contingent teachers and researchers are hired, evaluated, and promoted often bypass the faculty entirely and are generally less rigorous than the intense review applied to faculty in tenurable positions," as the 2009 AAUP report *Tenure and Teaching-Intensive Appointments* explains. It is by no means the contingent faculty member's fault that s/he does not undergo the process of becoming a peer by earning tenure. It's the fault of the vested members of universities—the TT faculty and administrators who let the academy grow dependent on casual hiring and low wages instead of investing in the kinds of processes and positions that confer professional legitimacy.

Far from being an elitist relic or a neoliberal fantasy, then, the tenure system works against the contemporary tide of expropriation. "All our experiences—as distinguished from theories and ideologies—tell us that the process of expropriation, which started with the rise of capitalism, does not stop with the expropriation of the means of production," Arendt wrote in 1970. "Only legal and political institutions that are independent of the economic forces and their automatism can control and check the inherently monstrous potentialities of this process."[25] The tenure system is built on precisely this logic, whereby the economic is disconnected from the legal and institutional so that the institution can function according to its own principles. When universities abandon this approach, they abandon their role as institutions intended to serve a free society.

If gestures of "democratic" inclusion unsupported by the accompanying practices of the academic profession are futile, then what are we to do? Ultimately, we agree with the AAUP report on NTT inclusion: the solution to the problems we've created over the past three decades is "not to bar some faculty from service but to better protect the academic freedom of those serving in governance roles." The critical question remains: how? And the answer is that we must build a tenure system for teaching-intensive faculty. The negative freedom of tenure—the freedom from pressure provided by job security—is the precondition for the positive freedom with which tenured faculty engage their peers (both other faculty and administrators). Is such freedom affordable for the majority of faculty today? Prestigious institutions, backed by the finance capital of their considerable endowments, can afford the modern university we like to imagine, one where faculty genuinely share governance with their partners in administration. How can we ensure that students who attend state universities have a professoriate with the same high level of independence enjoyed at elite institutions? What will it take to preserve and expand tenure at tuition-dependent institutions? If we make the effort, we can implement two different tracks offering eligibility to tenure along differentiated but commensurable lines. We can then winnow our adjunct numbers down to those people who fulfill the original template for the adjunct (professionals whose primary employment is elsewhere).

Hoping that academic freedom will continue to be protected so long as we remember to pay lip service to the ideal was never a strategy. It was an act of desperation. Now we need to do the hard work of rebuilding the profession by building procedures of professionalization for teaching faculty.

Notes

1. Michael Meranze, "We Wish We Weren't in Kansas Anymore: An Elegy for Academic Freedom," *Los Angeles Review of Books* 4 Mar. 2014. http://lareviewofbooks.org/essay/wish-werent-kansas-anymore-elegy-academic-freedom
2. *Tenure and Teaching-Intensive Appointments* (Washington, DC: American Association of University Professors, 2009). http://www.aaup.org/report/tenure-and-teaching-intensive-appointments
3. Berry, *Reclaiming the Ivory Tower*, p. 5.
4. Mary Burgan, *What Ever Happened to the Faculty? Drift and Decision in Higher Education* (Baltimore: Johns Hopkins University Press, 2006), p. 181.
5. John G. Cross and Edie N. Goldenberg, *Off-Track Profs: Nontenured Teachers in Higher Education* (Cambridge, MA: MIT Press, 2009), p. 8.
6. Menand, *The Future of Academic Freedom*, p. 3.
7. Peter Schmidt, "New Complaint to Accreditor Assails College's Treatment of Adjuncts," *Chronicle of Higher Education* 17 Apr. 2013. http://chronicle.com/article/New-Complaint-to-Accreditor/138555
8. Larry G. Gerber, "Professionalization as the Basis for Academic Freedom and Faculty Governance," *AAUP Journal of Academic Freedom* 1 (2010), p. 22.
9. "Declaration of Principles on Academic Freedom and Academic Tenure," Appendix I, *AAUP Policy Documents and Reports*, 10th ed. (Washington, DC: American Association of University Professors, 2006), p. 294.
10. Robert Post, "The Structure of Academic Freedom," in Beshara Doumani, ed., *Academic Freedom after September 11* (New York: Zone Books, 2006), p. 62.
11. Post, "The Structure of Academic Freedom," p. 64.
12. Gerber, "Professionalization as the Basis for Academic Freedom and Faculty Governance," p. 15.
13. *AAUP Policy Documents and Reports*, 11th ed. (Washington, DC: American Association of University Professors, 2015).
14. "Ramifications of the Supreme Court's Ruling in Garcetti v. Ceballos," Modern Language Association Committee on Academic Freedom and Professional Rights and Responsibilities. http://www.mla.org/garcetti_ceballos

15. Craig Calhoun, "Academic Freedom: Public Knowledge and the Structural Transformation of the University," *Social Research* 76.2 (2009), p. 571.
16. Meranze, "We Wish We Weren't in Kansas Anymore."
17. *The Inclusion in Governance of Faculty Members Holding Contingent Appointments* (Washington, DC: American Association of University Professors, 2012). http://www.aaup.org/report/governance-inclusion
18. Cary Nelson, *No University is an Island: Saving Academic Freedom* (New York University Press, 2010), p. 32.
19. Matthew Finkin and Robert Post, *For the Common Good: Principles of American Academic Freedom* (New Haven: Yale University Press, 2009), p. 33.
20. John Dewey, quoted in Finkin and Post, *For the Common Good*, p. 33.
21. Gerber, "Professionalization as the Basis for Academic Freedom and Faculty Governance," p. 21.
22. Menand, *The Future of Academic Freedom*, p. 4.
23. Bruce Robbins, "Outside Pressures," *Works and Days* 51/52, 53/54 (2008–9), p. 339.
24. Joan Wallach Scott, "Knowledge, Power, and Academic Freedom," *Social Research* 76.2 (2009), p. 460.
25. Hannah Arendt, *The Last Interview and Other Conversations* (New York: Melville House, 2013), p. 81.

4 On the Rails

Jennifer Ruth and Michael Bérubé

Michael:

The national leaders in the fight for contingent faculty rights are not well known. This is no surprise: we are talking about the leaders of loose coalitions of (mostly) unorganized and invisible faculty members, people unseen and unacknowledged even (or especially) by their own nominal departmental colleagues in the tenured ranks. It is only in the last two or three years that they have begun to become visible—and audible—as advocates for reform in higher education. Only rarely does the mainstream media (that is, outside the confines of the higher-ed press) feature the perspective of adjunct faculty: we can point to a *New York Times* story on J. D. Hoff of CUNY, a pair of PBS stories by (now former) adjunct professor Joe Fruscione, a searing *Washington Post* editorial ("Adjunct Professors Fight for Crumbs on Campus") by Colman McCarthy, and of course the coverage of the life and death of Margaret Mary Vojtko.[1] But we are counting on the fingers of one hand here. Very few people outside the precincts of academe know of the work of Joe Berry, president of the Coalition of Contingent Academic Labor (COCAL) and author of *Reclaiming the Ivory Tower*; or Maria Maisto, president of the New Faculty Majority (NFM); or Robert Samuels, president of the University of California-American Federation of Teachers and author of *Why Public Higher Education Should Be Free*; or Robin Sowards (also on the board of the NFM), who helped lead the fight to organize adjunct faculty at Duquesne as part of the Adjunct Faculty Association, affiliated (as is appropriate for Pittsburgh) with the

United Steelworkers of America. But we know of their work, and you should too. Much of what we argue in this book has been inspired by them, by precept and by example.

In 2012, thanks in part to his own ingenuity and in part to the wonders of the internet, Josh Boldt, then a young adjunct faculty member at the University of Georgia, suddenly joined the ranks of these unseen and unsung leaders. After reading my report on the January 2012 summit meeting of the New Faculty Majority in Washington,[2] which discussed the Modern Language Association's wage recommendations for contingent faculty (at the time, $6800/course), Boldt created "The Adjunct Project," an online crowdsourcing device that allowed contingent-faculty members to upload the details of their employment contracts—anonymously. The idea, of course, was that The Adjunct Project would reveal how many institutions (spoiler alert: *nearly all*) were falling short of MLA recommendations. As Boldt wrote:

> Almost $7K per course! Most adjuncts have never seen anything close to that figure. I personally have taught at schools that pay right at or below $2000 maximum per course. Feel free to do the math on that one (Hint: a 5/5 pays $20,000 annually). You can be a terrible human being and still recognize that a full-time teacher should earn much more than that. Just in case you're not familiar with the usual procedure, full-time professors generally teach much less than 10 courses per year. Some teach as few as three. The MLA's recommendation is based on the assumption of a 3/3 teaching load, which sounds about perfect. I would venture to say most adjuncts would agree. Three courses per semester is ideal because it allows teaching to be the primary focus (as it should be), and it also permits some time for research and professional development. So, about $40,000 a year. That isn't too much to ask I don't think. Especially considering all adjuncts have advanced degrees in their fields....

In light of this new pay recommendation, I've decided to start collecting data about how many schools come close to this standard. By making this information public, we can recognize the schools that are doing a great job (like my school, the University of Georgia, for example). They deserve to be patted on the back for their good work. On the other hand, we will also be able expose those schools that have chosen to ignore the basic human rights of their employees and shortchange their students and their communities by devaluing the very education they pretend to celebrate.[3]

Boldt's "Adjunct Project" went viral, and was soon picked up by the *Chronicle of Higher Education*; I responded, during my one-year term as MLA President in 2012, by asking Boldt, Maisto, Samuels, and MLA Committee on Contingent Labor in the Profession (CLIP) co-chair Elizabeth Landers to present papers at the Presidential Forum of the MLA's annual convention.

At that Presidential Forum, Boldt mounted an argument very much like the argument of this book:

The new career track for university faculty members is that of the disposable professor. As we rely more and more on adjunct labor, we slowly surrender our power on college campuses. Contingent faculty members are powerless. Replaceable. No tenure, no bargaining rights, no contract, no voice. Adjuncts—who are faculty members—become products for consumption in this new free-market university economy that, like the free-market business economy, places the bottom line above all else.

What effect does this powerlessness have on important concepts like academic integrity and freedom?[4]

As we have argued in these pages, the effect is devastating. But perhaps it is so devastating that it might lead some contingent faculty members (and their advocates) to sever the link between tenure and academic freedom, or abandon the notion of tenure altogether, settling instead for more short-term improvements in salary and job security that will make precarious faculty positions considerably less precarious.[5]

Jennifer:

Fittingly, one of the most thoughtful and eloquent voices in that debate has been that of Josh Boldt himself. In a 2014 *Chronicle of Higher Education* forum on the future of tenure ("what discussions will we be having about tenure in 10 years?"), Boldt responded emphatically, in an essay cheekily titled "99 Problems But Tenure Ain't One":

> Where will tenure be in 10 years? No adjunct professor should care. Here's why:
> Most non-tenure-track professors couldn't even say where they'll be in 10 weeks, let alone 10 years. Asking an adjunct to support tenure is like asking a homeless person to support a tax deduction for homeowners.

Boldt references his MLA Presidential Forum paper in a hyperlink, noting (justly) that he is "an outspoken proponent of collaboration between tenure-track and non-tenure-track professors." But the premise of his "99 Problems" essay is that contingent faculty have no stake whatsoever in the tenure system:

> What we're really talking about when we talk about tenure is a very small and ever-dwindling privileged group. Instead, I want to focus on the needs of the needy. Better pay, health insurance, longer contracts: These are the pressing concerns of the vast majority, and they should take precedent as we work to fix our broken system.
> As for fixing that system, I'd advocate for arrangements that give decent salaries, benefits, and five-year contracts to most professors before I would negotiate to perpetuate a

tenure system in which the poor majority works to support the more comfortable minority.

What I'm trying to say here is if we want to find a common interest in the fight to save our profession, preserving tenure is not it. It's too narrow and too irrelevant to too many people. We should instead focus on goals that benefit more universal needs of the academic community. With the rise of adjunct unions, these needs will soon become the priority, like it or not. I hope our tenured colleagues want to work together and share our goals.[6]

The problem with this argument is that it is right. Under current conditions, non-tenure-track faculty members have no hope whatsoever of escaping the system of at-whim employment, and they have no reason to feel anything but resentment or indifference toward the "lifeboaters" who managed to luck into the few remaining tenured positions from which they can watch the ship sink. The needs of the needy, obviously, take priority: if there are no more lifeboats, then more and better life preservers are called for.

Accordingly, attempts to reform our institutions from the periphery—that is, from the least enfranchised, though not the minority—are so far proving the most powerful mechanism for change. We agree with Boldt that the rise of adjunct unions (as well as AAUP's redoubled efforts in collective bargaining) will make higher salaries, benefits, and extended contracts the priority for institutions whether they "like it or not." If there is any bite in Boldt's "like it or not," this is only fair. Tenured faculty have had enough time to work on this problem—but so far, we have not used our own hard-won independence to preserve the possibility of independence for others. As we argued earlier, we could have used our freedom to say that we won't grow by expanding the ranks of the exploited. We can still do this. And we can answer Boldt's argument: we can and must do the hard and inescapably painful work of building a teaching-intensive tenure track.

Better contracts and salaries for contingent faculty would be an improvement, yes. And it is entirely reasonable for contingent faculty living on sub-subsistence wages to focus on goals that appear achievable in the course of a single year, through collective bargaining or otherwise. Over the long term, however, there is no substitute for the institution of tenure. We are joined in this belief by the American Association of University Professors, whose *Tenure and Teaching-Intensive Appointments* report holds that "the best way to stabilize the faculty infrastructure is to bundle the employment and economic securities that activist faculty on contingent appointments are already winning for themselves with the rigorous scrutiny of the tenure system."[7] With adjunct unions at the forefront of change, we may well see employment and economic securities improve, and again, this alone would be sufficient for the short term. But the other critical component of professionalism—the autonomy earned through professions' self-policing mechanisms—may continue to atrophy. The struggle for better basic working conditions will have been won (at some campuses, perhaps), but the broader struggle for meaningful shared governance and academic freedom will have been lost.

Tenured faculty and administrators—those "vested" members we've been talking about—are obliged to think of the state of academic employment over the long term. This is because tenure empowers faculty in ways that better pay and benefits alone do not. We, for example, do not feel that we work for our respective PSU (Penn State University and Portland State University) presidents. Having gone through the tenure process, we work for our discipline, our colleagues, and our students. No doubt this will strike people who are convinced that all faculty are managed by despotic administrators as naïve or idealistic. But it is, nonetheless, a conviction that has empowered us in shared governance on our campuses time and again, allowing us to contribute to, and comment critically on, university policies governing everything from faculty/staff benefits to email-use policy to the general education curriculum for undergraduate students.

No doubt there are others who will view our conviction not so much as naïve as self-indulgent. As far as this group is concerned, we *should* consider ourselves management's employees, since otherwise we are likely to be Roger Kimball's tenured radicals, exempting ourselves from all accountability. As Michael noted in the Introduction, there is probably no way to make the case for tenure and academic freedom to people who oppose tenure on principle. And there are people on both the right and the left (though it is an addled wing of the left) who insist that professors are no different from any other kind of employee; they are not special snowflakes in need of extra protection (for some reason the phrase "special snowflakes" is invoked in 95 percent of these discussions). The irony here is that the tenure system demands a high degree of accountability and works to cultivate in faculty a deep sense of responsibility to their discipline and students. In *Higher Education in America,* former Harvard president Derek Bok offers a defense of tenure for the anti-tenure set; indeed, it is clear that the defense is aimed at the anti-tenure set because it is so patently half-hearted. Bok sounds as weary as the next administrator with the privileges tenure confer on faculty, and yet he explains on very pragmatic grounds why the tenure track remains for him the preferable model for the professoriate:

> Doing away with tenure might ... weaken the standards for hiring and promoting faculty. Appointing a professor for life is such a consequential matter for a department that even softhearted faculty members will insist on a high standard of work before voting in favor. If the prevailing system were replaced, say, by a practice of making appointments for only five years, faculties might well be less inclined to be tough-minded and more prepared to give younger candidates the benefit of any reasonable doubts. Once such a person had

been reappointed for two or three terms, tenured colleagues and other senior professors might hesitate for compassionate reasons to recommend against reappointment, especially in fields where rejected scholars in their forties or fifties would be hard put to find alternative employment.[8]

Bok's thinking here rings true. Few people are willing to fire (or not renew) someone when the alternative exists to punt the judgment down the line to others. The absence of the tenure system, in other words, leads to *less* accountability—and this is *precisely* what has happened over the past few decades.

Let's return to the Ad Hoc Committee on Fixed-Term Faculty discussed in the first half of Chapter 3, the committee that blew up so spectacularly. Whereas I had hoped the committee would develop a path to promotion for teaching-intensive faculty, instead the committee members could not give up on the idea that research should be an essential component of any college professor's portfolio. I was disappointed but I understood. I, too, wish public universities were funded at the Sputnik-era rates that allowed the majority of positions to bundle teaching, research, and service. As it is, though, fewer than 30 percent of professors still enjoy such jobs. We need to demand that states recommit to public higher education, of course; we need to make the case to legislators, as we argued in the Introduction, that what has happened on that front amounts to one generation's betrayal of another. Nevertheless, any plausible plan for reform needs to work at least loosely within current economic constraints if we want it to be implemented immediately—and if we want it to endure for the long term.

It was driven home to me how difficult it is to digest the brute economic facts when I sat down with Portland State University's numbers. I had long known that my university reflects the national trends, and yet I persisted half-consciously and irrationally to assume that only a few PSU departments in the liberal arts were responsible for the unhappy statistics.

In fact, here's how the division of labor plays out in five of Portland State's main colleges: In the College of the Liberal Arts, 34% of student credit hours (SCH) are taught by TT faculty, 28% by full-time NTT faculty, and 30% by adjuncts. In the College of the Arts, the corresponding numbers are 38%, 13%, and 47%. In the College of Urban and Public Affairs, they are 40%, 35%, and 22%. In the School of Social Work: 32%, 26%, and 30%. The School of Business Administration: 25%, 28%, and 46%. (The numbers don't add up to 100% because I dropped the percentages taught by graduate students.) There are, to be sure, some interesting variations here but this much is obvious—the casualization of faculty has happened *in all sectors of the university* not just in the humanities.

Michael:

It remains unclear to me why the humanities have taken the lead in this discussion—or, perhaps, taken it on the chin. Perhaps we were the first disciplines whose faculty were casualized; perhaps we were the first to notice. Perhaps we have a higher percentage of outspoken labor activists, such as Marc Bousquet, who sounded the alarm about contingent faculty as early as 20 years ago. Be that as it may, Jennifer's numbers are real, and other disciplines are beginning to catch on. Witness this 2014 article in the online journal *BioScience*:

> According to 2011 data from the National Center for Education Statistics (the most recent available), just under 30 percent of higher-education faculty members today are tenured or on the tenure track. In contrast, in 1969, 78 percent of faculty members were tenured or tenure track, and less than 22 percent were not. The majority of today's non-tenure-track faculty members are low-paid part-timers, whose working conditions often adversely affect learning outcomes for students.
>
> "In the biology department at Rowan University, it is possible for a freshman biology major to go their entire 4 years for a bachelor's of science without taking a course taught

by a tenure-track professor," says Nathan Ruhl, an adjunct professor at the Glassboro, New Jersey-based school.

"That's actually frightening," says AIBS [American Institute of Biological Sciences] Board member Muriel Poston, dean of faculty at Pitzer College, in Claremont, California. The shift to contingency and away from tenured faculty couldn't have come at a worse time, she says. "It's a confluence of some really challenging events: increasing numbers of students interested in science, particularly in biology, and increasing numbers of underrepresented groups, just when there's a significant shift in the teaching population [from tenured to contingent]."

One leading researcher on contingent academic employment endorses the idea that the humanities were the canaries in the coal mine:

"It used to be [that], primarily, the big growth [in adjunct faculty] was in the humanities," says Adrianna Kezar, professor of education at the University of Southern California and director of the Delphi Project on Changing Faculty and Student Success. "But mathematics is full of adjuncts, and in biology, the number is starting to grow—anything with large introductory courses, which includes biology, chemistry, and mathematics. It's across all types of institutions. My own university has over 50 percent adjuncts, and we're in the [top] 100 elite universities. It doesn't matter what institution, what discipline—contingency is across all."[9]

As these numbers demonstrate, the overwhelming majority of faculty in the classroom are not being paid to do research. We need to be able to professionalize and stabilize these faculty without using the standards we rely upon to evaluate faculty from whom research is expected. We need to implement teaching-intensive tenure tracks. "Should more classroom teaching be done by faculty supported by the rigorous peer scrutiny of the tenure system?" asks the 2009 AAUP report on teaching-intensive appointments. "Most of the evidence says yes, and a host of diverse voices agree," it answers. To critics who might object that a teaching-intensive tenure track creates a two-tier system, one for research faculty and one for what some institutions call "professors of the practice," we can only say yes, yes it does. And we would add that our two-tiered tenure system is vastly preferable to the vicious, unstable three-tier system we live in now.

Jennifer:

For as long as it has been possible to pay full-time NTT faculty and adjuncts significantly lower wages, administrators and tenured faculty have been able to maintain high levels of denial about what this system entails and how it works. Because pay for contingent faculty has taken up so little of the budget, they managed to tell themselves that they don't really rely *that much* on contingent faculty, even as the majority of the SCH in their tuition-driven budgets are taught by faculty off the tenure track. As the strikes in 2014 at Portland State and the University of Illinois at Chicago (both of which involved NTT/TT coalitions) indicate, this kind of denial is no longer possible. Universities will be forced to invest more in these faculty positions and, once they do, casual hiring will become increasingly unacceptable. Why would an institution exempt a newly expensive workforce from the accountability it has always expected from its old expensive workforce?

Michael:

We want to make it very clear that we are not suggesting that contingent faculty members themselves are unprofessional. That is not the problem. The problem is that *they are not treated as professionals*—from the moment they are hired, to positions in which they lack access to offices, phones, email, libraries, and even parking, to the moment they are given summary notice that their services will not be required next term. This is the problem addressed by the 2011 report of the Modern

Language Association's Committee on Contingent Labor in the Profession, *Professional Employment Practices for Non-Tenure-Track Faculty Members: Recommendations and Evaluative Questions*. It is a document which every department, in every discipline, should have on hand—and abide by. (It is not hard to download and distribute in a department near you; it is only four pages long.)[10] But the point remains that faculty off the tenure track are generally not hired or renewed (or fired) with the same level of rigorous scrutiny applied to their tenured colleagues. The institutions that employ them do not invest that kind of time and energy into their professionalization; and conversely, contingent faculty have no reason to invest significant time and energy in the long-term health of the institutions that employ them.

Jennifer:

As we mentioned in Chapter 3, the AAUP chapter at Portland State passed equity-at-rank minimums for TT and NTT faculty. This past year, the salary floors were raised again. Table 1 shows the salary minimums agreed upon in the Collective Bargaining Agreement (CBA) for 2014 to 2015. Portland State is well within the ballpark of the MLA's wage recommendations for full-time faculty. Its adjunct pay remains deplorable, however. This clearly needs to be the next push, ideally through a coalition between the union representing full-time faculty (PSU-AAUP) and the one representing adjunct instructors (PSUFA-AFT). Since Portland State already invests financially in its *full-time* NTT faculty, transitioning this workforce to the tenure track is more of a logistical and cultural shift than it is an economic nightmare. Accordingly, I and my colleague Amy Greenstadt developed a scenario that we believe would be effective in making this shift, and we offer it here as the Appendix. The idea is that while each university's circumstances differ, some of what Amy and I worked out will be portable to other institutions.

This is a plan pitched with administrators in mind as its audience. We hope to convince them to implement this

Table 1 Salary minimums for Portland State faculty members, 2014–15

Rank	9-month appt. 1 Feb. 2014	12-month appt. 1 Jan. 2014
Professor	$80,748	$98,520
Clinical or Professor of Practice	80,748	98,520
Associate Professor	65,637	80,088
Associate Clinical or Professor of Practice	65,637	80,088
Assistant Professor	54,918	67,008
Assistant Clinical Professor or Professor of Practice	54,918	67,008
Senior Instructor II	53,820	65,664
Senior Instructor I	45,603	55,644
Instructor	40,005	48,816
Senior Research Associate II	49,554	60,456
Senior Research Associate I	45,774	55,848
Research Associate	43,812	53,472
Senior Research Assistant II	42,733	52,140
Senior Research Assistant I	40,698	49,656
Research Assistant	40,005	48,816

model or something very much like it. Administrators who have experienced the kind of strife we experienced recently at Portland State are more likely to be open to such proposals. At institutions where top administrators have yet to apprehend the way stepped-up union activity has changed the game, Faculty Senates will be the place to articulate and push through similar plans. A number of Faculty Senates have already been very active on this front. (See the Senate webpages for University of Colorado at Boulder—in particular, their Final Task Force Report of 2010—and the University of Oregon.)

Jennifer and Michael:

Finally, we must say a word about the pain that is inevitable in our proposal for reform. There are a lot of bad reasons why administrators and TT faculty have done nothing about the crisis, and why the burden of change has fallen too heavily on the activism of the least-empowered faculty group. We've talked about many of these bad reasons in this book. There is, however, one *good* reason why the empowered constituencies have done so little even when they have not been paralyzed or fatalistic: because any considered and sustainable change is unlikely to accommodate all the individuals who by rights deserve to be accommodated. It turns out that bucking the system that is already in place is going to be almost as hard on the conscience as maintaining it is. Even if in the long run better jobs with access to tenure are created, and this improves the university (and, in turn, society) by strengthening academic freedom, particular persons will lose out. No matter how ingenious the circumstances designed to move us from a majority off-track to majority on-track workforce, no matter how irreproachably conscientious, there will be outcomes that feel—and undoubtedly are—unjust from one perspective or another.

The proposal in the Appendix makes it possible for many NTT faculty to be converted to a teaching-intensive tenure track, and as we eliminate NTT positions, we advocate replacing them with TT hires in regional or national searches. The NTT faculty who were hired ad hoc will be eligible to apply for those positions—but inevitably, those faculty members who do not possess terminal degrees will be at a disadvantage in such searches, which will of course draw many applicants (regionally or nationally) with terminal degrees, including those people with terminal degrees who already work as adjunct instructors at the institutions. We expect, therefore, that our proposal will be seen in some quarters as elitist, privileging PhD holders over the legions of MAs and ABDs (people who have completed all requirements but for their dissertations) now occupying NTT positions. Our proposal does indeed privilege PhD holders. But this is not elitism; it is *professionalism*. Marc Bousquet puts it well in *How the University Works*: when "degree holding no longer represents control over who may practice," the result is "a failed monopoly of professional labor."[11] As early as 1998, in fact, Bousquet argued that disciplinary associations like the MLA had an obligation to promote this kind of professionalism: "Graduate students," he told the *Chronicle of Higher Education*, "need the MLA to make sure that people holding Ph.D. degrees are doing the teaching in today's college classrooms."[12] The only problem with this is that the MLA, unlike the American Bar Association or the American Medical Association, is not a credentializing or credential-checking body. It has no means of enforcing any edict about faculty members who do not hold terminal degrees, no power to fire thousands of non-PhDs across the country. The profession devolved into academic serfdom and patronage systems department by department, hire by hire, and this is how we will have to turn it around. This book has examined how difficult it will be: constraints on our time, our funds, and our energy must be overcome; our personal commitments and interpersonal variables can make judgment-making particularly fraught. There is no doubt in our minds, however, that reform is both possible and necessary. Insofar as the PhD is a credential for college teaching, then we should be treating the PhD as a credential for college teaching in all regional and national searches—excepting only those fields where the MFA is the terminal degree—and "privileging" it accordingly in conversions to the teaching-intensive tenure track. As Bousquet insists, the academic job market does not overproduce PhDs; it *underhires* PhDs. Any meaningful reform of the academic job system must address this.

Michael:

That's the difficult part: not everyone hired ad hoc can expect to be grandfathered into a teaching-intensive tenure track. The AAUP holds, as a matter of principle, that all contingent faculty members with more than six years of service should be considered to have the same academic due process protections as tenure; but unlike almost all AAUP principles, this one is ignored by the vast majority of colleges and universities. And yet some provision must be made, some consideration must be given, for senior NTT faculty in their forties, fifties, or sixties with far more than six years of continuous employment at one institution; many of them are accomplished, seasoned teachers who should certainly be asked to continue serving as accomplished, seasoned teachers—at better wages. But ultimately, if academe does move toward a two-track tenure system as we suggest, some NTT faculty will be jeopardized. In an essay for the MLA journal *Profession*, Beth Landers discusses her experience on the MLA's Committee on Contingent Labor in the Profession, confronting precisely this issue:

> What each of us considered to be progress or good news for contingent labor also varied considerably: for example, when a community college administrator proudly shared the news that her school had just eliminated a number of non-tenure-track positions in order to create a larger number of tenure-track positions with benefits, a committee member working off the tenure track confessed that this scenario was his worst nightmare, because it meant that many NTT faculty like himself were likely to be out of a job.[13]

Landers's essay includes a detailed account of how the University of Missouri system created protocols and procedures for the review—and promotion—of NTT faculty; we suggest that other systems, *mutatis mutandis*, could adopt similar policies, though we insist that any regularization of the NTT faculty ranks should come with a path to a teaching-intensive tenure track. Landers argues that because the conditions of contingent labor differ so dramatically within and across institutions, all solutions and reforms must be local in character, fitted to the contours of idiosyncratic employment practices from department to department, institution to institution. We might add that the very nature of shared governance, which takes such different forms at different colleges and universities, will ensure that reform will look different on different campuses. We are aware that not every institution will give priority to PhDs in the way we suggest, and some will counter that the MA is, for them, a sufficiently advanced degree for a teaching-intensive position. Nonetheless, we urge the bottom line that university administrators and faculty work to convince their campuses to adopt a teaching-intensive tenure track that is built and maintained through open, fair searches. Faculty who focus on teaching and are not evaluated for research must have access to academic freedom in all they do—and, critically, the ability to participate fully *and freely* in shared governance.

Before we close this chapter, we want to answer one question: *why should we bother?* Why should academe be saved? Why shouldn't it be allowed to go the way of so many other areas of American life? Why shouldn't it be subject to the same kinds of depredations experienced by the airline industry, by nurses, by service workers? More and more forms of employment have become "precarious," as *micro-entrepreneur, flexploitation*, and the hideous euphemism *the sharing economy* have become the watchwords of our times. In a world of flexible just-in-time labor, with its Airbnbs and Ubers and Lyfts and Handybooks and TaskRabbits and Instacarts, why shouldn't higher education get with the program? Why shouldn't your phone have an app for summoning a course, or perhaps just a lecture or two, on Hellenistic culture or introductory physics?

Conservative attacks on higher education, together with the Bitter Lamentation Chorus of people like William Deresiewicz, have helped to obscure the extraordinary accomplishments of American higher education since 1945. Beginning in the early postwar period and extending through the era of the Civil Rights Movement and the entry of women into the professions, the United States undertook an experiment in mass higher education. This experiment, the first in the world's history, helped build a middle class that was also unprecedented in world history; indeed, over the past four decades, the retrenchment of the one has accompanied and abetted the retrenchment of the other. The American system became, and despite its deepening flaws still remains, the envy of the world. Higher education is one of the few areas of contemporary life in which the United States enjoys a considerable trade surplus, so to speak, as international students arrive from around the globe for education and training. But all that has been badly eroded now, and a university system that should be the centerpiece of a free society has been gradually transformed into a patchwork enterprise where the majority of professors are hired on a piecework, just-in-time basis at sub-subsistence wages. The damage is irreparable in the sense that we are never going back to that golden age of postwar expansion. But it is not inevitable, and ostensibly urgent analyses of academic labor that blame the global forces of neoliberalism have the ultimately reassuring subtext that none of this is our fault, that we are all the playthings of the winds of austerity. The damage is in fact the result of decisions made department by department, institution by institution, and that is how reform must proceed as well.

Faculty working conditions are student learning conditions. To employ a large cohort of disposable professors without offices, phones, or access to email is not only inhumane to the professors themselves but also a profound insult to students—and to everyone who cares about students. It is a bitter irony that most of the discussions of higher education, in official and political circles, call on universities to become more "accountable." Most of these calls are the work of people who want to see quantifiable "learning outcomes" and are trying to extend the brutal, reductive logic of high-stakes testing beyond the K-12 system, where it has already warped so much of the mission of education. But there is a sense in which universities *should* be more accountable—accountable to all the constituencies, students first and foremost, who have a stake in ensuring that professors have professional working conditions. Universities worthy of the name, then, must become accountable to the idea and the ideals of professionalism—and accrediting agencies must begin to measure them that way. This is not, we realize, as rousing a cry as "workers of the world unite," and there will inevitably be workers who decide that they do not have a stake in it. But everyone who is interested in the future of higher education, and everyone who understands the *real* crisis undermining the integrity of the institution, should support the effort to expand the professional domain of tenure and academic freedom to all qualified faculty. From the debates about the nature of universalism in the humanities to the debates about the nature of the universe in the sciences, the university is an institution worth saving—one institution at a time.

Notes

1. For Hoff, see Rachel L. Swarns, "Crowded Out of Ivory Tower, Adjuncts See a Life Less Lofty," *New York Times* 19 Jan. 2014. http://www.nytimes.com/2014/01/20/nyregion/crowded-out-of-ivory-tower-adjuncts-see-a-life-less-lofty.html?_r=0; for Fruscione, see "When a College Contracts 'Adjunctivitis,' It's the Students Who Lose," *PBS Newshour: Making Sen$e*. 25 Jul. 2014. http://www.pbs.org/newshour/making-sense/when-a-college-contracts-adjunctivitis-its-the-students-who-lose/; and "What Parents Need to Know About College Faculty," *PBS Newshour: Making Sen$e* 14 Aug. 2014. http://www.pbs.org/newshour/making-sense/what-parents-need-to-know-about-college-faculty/; for McCarthy, see "Adjunct Professors Fight for Crumbs on Campus," *Washington Post* 22 Aug. 2014. http://www.washingtonpost.com/opinions/adjunct-professors-fight-for-crumbs-on-campus/2014/08/22/ca92eb38-28b1-11e4-8593-da634b334390_story.html
2. Michael Bérubé, "Among the Majority," *Modern Language Association: From the President* 1 Feb. 2012. http://www.mla.org/fromthepres&topic=146
3. Josh Boldt, "Crowdsourcing a Compilation of Adjunct Working Conditions," *Order of Education* 2 Feb. 2012. http://orderofeducation.com/crowdsourcing-a-compilation-of-adjunct-working-conditions/
4. Josh Boldt, "Free-Market Faculty Members," *Profession 2013*. New York: Modern Language Association. http://profession.commons.mla.org/2013/10/08/free-market-faculty-members/
5. One plan for long-term improvement in salary and job security has a good deal of support among contingent faculty activists: it is

usually referred to as the Vancouver Plan, and it was drafted by Jack Longmate and Frank Cosco, based largely on Cosco's experience at Vancouver Community College (its official title is "Program for Change: 2010–2030"). Longmate serves on the Board of Directors of the New Faculty Majority, and Cosco serves on the Advisory Board. Their plan has a great deal to recommend it: it is a thoughtful, judicious proposal for radically reducing the ranks of contingent faculty incrementally over 20 years, and for conducting the business of academic labor on the principle that all university teachers deserve fair and equal treatment. Jennifer and I, however, have offered an alternative model for two reasons. First, and most important, the Vancouver Plan does not have a teaching-intensive tenure track; on the contrary, it proposes that "eventually tenure be delinked from salary and time-status." It is based on a collective bargaining model in which job security is a matter of contracts rather than of tenure and academic freedom, and on a British Columbia system that involves "normalization" or "regularization" of faculty members after a probationary period. Those models are undoubtedly superior to the broken system under which we now operate, but, as we hope we have made clear, we believe there is finally no substitute for tenure. Second, the Vancouver Plan operates on the assumption that all faculty members have been hired through fair, open, and competitive processes. To put this another way, it makes no distinction between faculty hired by means of professional mechanisms of peer review and faculty hired ad hoc. It therefore does not address the practices that have undermined professional systems of review in higher education. That said, Longmate and Cosco do acknowledge that the plan is "not meant to be prescriptive or proscriptive and that we could not imagine seriously presenting the Program in its entirety for immediate adoption anywhere," and Jennifer and I agree with much of its spirit if not with its every detail.

6. Josh Boldt, "99 Problems But Tenure Ain't One," *Chronicle Vitae (Chronicle of Higher Education)* 21 Jan. 2014. https://chroniclevitae.com/news/283-99-problems-but-tenure-ain-t-one
7. *Tenure and Teaching-Intensive Appointments*. Washington, DC: American Association of University Professors, 2009. http://www.aaup.org/report/tenure-and-teaching-intensive-appointments
8. Derek Bok, *Higher Education in America* (Princeton University Press, 2013), p. 365.
9. Beth Baker, "The End of the Academy?" *BioScience* 64.8 (2014): 647–652. http://bioscience.oxfordjournals.org/content/64/8/647.full
10. And it is readily available on an internet near you: *Professional Employment Practices for Non-Tenure-Track Faculty Members: Recommendations*

and Evaluative Questions. MLA Committee on Contingent Labor in the Profession. New York: Modern Language Association, 2011. http://www.mla.org/pdf/clip_stmt_final_may11.pdf

11. Marc Bousquet, *How the University Works: Higher Education and the Low-Wage Nation* (New York University Press, 2008), p. 23.
12. Bousquet, quoted in Courtney Leatherman and Robin Wilson, "Embittered by a Bleak Job Market, Graduate Students Take on the MLA," 18 Dec. 1998. https://chronicle.com/article/Embittered-by-a-Bleak-Job/30852
13. Elizabeth Landers, "Contingent Labor: National Perspectives, Local Solutions," *Profession 2013*. http://profession.commons.mla.org/2013/10/08/contingent-labor-national-perspectives-local-solutions/

Appendix: Implementing a Teaching-Intensive Tenure Track at Portland State University

The university publicly announces a plan to immediately stabilize the employment of a large percentage of the PSU faculty by converting the positions of Senior Instructor from NTT to TT.

- All Senior Instructors who were hired through regional or national competitive searches will become eligible for tenure in 3 years. Their job titles and duties will remain largely the same (i.e., focused on instruction). At the 3-year mark, they will either receive tenure or their employment with PSU will be terminated and their positions will be open to new applicants.
- Those Senior Instructor positions currently occupied by employees who were "fast-tracked," or not initially hired through regional or national competitive searches, will be eliminated and replaced with tenure-track Senior Instructor positions. These positions will then be advertised and filled through regional or national competitive searches. Faculty whose employment was terminated as a result of this change will be invited to apply for the new tenure-track positions.
- *Exception*: Senior Instructors who have been continuously employed at PSU since September 2008 and who were not hired in competitive searches **may keep their current positions** or transition to tenure-track positions and become eligible for tenure in 3 years. If they choose the second option their job titles and duties will remain largely

the same (i.e., focused on instruction). At the 3-year mark, they will either receive tenure or their employment with PSU will be terminated and their positions will be open to new applicants.
- NTTF who have been grandfathered as Assistant/Associate/Full Professors and whose job duties and qualifications are commensurate with those of Senior Instructors will have the following options:
  - If hired in a competitive search or employed continuously at PSU since 2008, they may keep their current positions and titles or transition to tenure-track positions **in the Senior Instructor track** and become eligible for tenure in 3 years (they must change job title).
  - If not hired in a competitive search or employed continuously at PSU since 2008, their position will be discontinued and replaced with a tenure-track Senior Instructor position to which they will be invited to apply as part of a regional or national search.
- The university *will not* reduce the total number of full-time faculty it employs as a result of this process.

At the same time, the university will issue press releases and internal communications to explain the above actions, citing these reasons:

- Job security for faculty is necessary to foster innovation in teaching, research, and university governance. To be competitive in the 21st century, we need a faculty with the security to take risks and develop new strategies in delivering cutting-edge, high-quality, and affordable education in Oregon.
- This administration considers robust shared governance to be one of the most important ingredients of a healthy university. Expanding access to tenure will increase the percentage of faculty who can engage in shared governance with confidence.

Appendix

- This administration considers academic freedom to be the legitimating principle of the American university. As universities increasingly relied on off-tenure faculty, academic freedom at these institutions has been diminished. It is time to correct this and restore faculty autonomy and integrity.
- The old model of tenure was based on the idea that faculty would divide their time evenly between research and teaching; while the university still needs faculty to teach advanced scholarship in their fields, the increased demand for higher education and explosion in our student population necessitate that we include faculty whose primary responsibility is instruction, and who are especially expert in helping students develop basic knowledge and skills in their disciplines. While up until now PSU, like most US universities, has hired these faculty on a temporary and often casual basis, it has become clear that this practice hurts students and the university as a whole. Only faculty with job security can participate freely in the academic life of their institutions and larger scholarly communities.
- To ensure this high quality and enrich faculty members' sense of belonging to the university community, it is necessary that these faculty members be hired in competitive searches. In the past, the university has too often hired on a casual basis and this practice needs to cease and its consequences, to the extent possible, corrected. Hiring competitively will also give the university's large part-time faculty workforce, many of whom have been teaching at PSU for several years, the opportunity to compete for full-time, tenure-track jobs.
- However, the university recognizes the invaluable contributions of faculty who have taught here for many years. Their years of excellent service demonstrate their value, even if they were not initially hired in competitive searches. Although in general it is more fair to open valuable faculty positions to competitive searches, in the case of these

faculty it is more fair to allow them to retain their positions or have the option to transition to tenure-track positions.
- To demonstrate its commitment to the academic quality that comes with tenure, the university is instituting a new, rigorous post-tenure review process to ensure that job security increases, rather than encourages, a dynamic approach to higher education. The university is also instituting new training programs for tenure-line faculty in university governance, so that the institution's direction can become increasingly faculty-driven and therefore responsive to the needs of students and the larger scholarly/professional community.

Bottom lines

The above scenario puts the university administration in the lead position. However, faculty will and should have the right to negotiate its terms, whether through faculty governance or collective bargaining. We have purposely built flexibility into the terms above, therefore. However, we believe the university's bottom lines should be the following:

- No faculty who have been at PSU less than 7 years will automatically be eligible for tenure; their jobs must be terminated and replaced with tenure-track positions open to competitive searches. In many cases, full-time NTT faculty do not hold terminal degrees in their field. Casual hiring kept many jobs out of reach of qualified applicants. This significantly weakened the job market in many disciplines. We owe it to the graduate students in those disciplines as well as our own students to open these positions to all qualified applicants.
- The stringent "up or out" moment of tenure is retained. Because the university is giving an extraordinary degree of job security to those it tenures, the bar must be high for the system to possess legitimacy for those involved as well as

for outside stakeholders (students, parents, the community). Faculty who have undergone an "eye of the needle" evaluation will in turn enforce a high standard when they are in a position to evaluate their peers. Having been successful in achieving tenure, they will be better able to see themselves as fully entitled members of the university community, which will mitigate the perceived need for adversarial collective negotiations.

Why specify regional or national searches?

In making similar reforms about a decade ago, the University of Oregon stipulated that all "career NTTF" be hired through national searches. We want to include the possibility of regional searches, however, because we believe that this will give PSU's adjunct population an enhanced opportunity to compete for full-time, tenure-track positions. There are many long-term (adjunct) faculty at PSU who have not been treated fairly because they have been shut out of competitive searches for full-time positions.

The hiring process must involve a committee and as much departmental participation as possible. One of the perceived and real problems with casual hiring of NTTF is that the instructor's relationship is often with an individual (usually, the chair) and not with the department as a whole. This encourages a patronage culture. Conversely, TT faculty often resent the chair's ability to staff the schedule with people she or he has handpicked. To avoid these problems and generate a sense of legitimacy for both the individual faculty member and the department at large, a committee and some substantial degree of department participation in the hire will be expected. The hiring of TT senior instructors should parallel the intensive process undertaken when the department has hired TTF in the past. This will add some cost but is crucial if the culture is going to improve. This will also add considerable labor. We will have to think about how to reassure departments who do not feel they have time to undertake this level of due diligence. (The fact that very little department labor is involved in hiring casually has been one of the reasons for our increasing reliance on casual hires.)

Evaluations for tenure will include extra-departmental assessments of teaching. This means that people outside the person's department—either from another department at PSU that is within the same 'family' (humanities, social sciences, etc.)—or from another institution provide evaluations of the person's teaching materials and teaching. This is critical for two reasons: (A) There can be no perception of corruption, no sense that friends are evaluating friends (and people in the same department often become or are perceived to be friends). The person evaluated by people s/he does not know will feel legitimated by a good evaluation and will be less able to argue that foul play was involved if given a negative evaluation. (B) In order to reframe the narrative from one about "two classes of university citizens, the elite and the proletariat," we launch a narrative about two tracks of faculty, those excellent in conventional jobs and those who excel in teaching. The teaching workforce—the Senior Instructor I and II—are valued for their excellent teaching at a university that is still as much about teaching and access as it is about research. When we try to make the claim in our current environment that we value teaching just as much as research, this rings false because we do not systematically evaluate teaching in a way comparable to the way we evaluate research for tenure (through outside review). Outside evaluations of teaching will go a long way toward increasing the prestige—and status—of teaching and we believe that this, in turn, will improve the culture.

Will the tenure-track positions differ from the previous NTT positions?

We believe it is important for the job duties of these positions to remain largely the same, even as they are converted from NTT to TT, both so that faculty currently in those positions will have an optimal chance of success, and because the university needs faculty positions with high teaching loads. However, the TT positions will need to incorporate university service explicitly, whereas currently NTT positions do not require service. Our current recommendation is that the tenure-track Senior Instructor positions stipulate that 10 percent of faculty workload be devoted to service (this is the current maximum for NTTF provided in the CBA).

Because service will be part of the expectations for tenure-track Senior Instructors, we believe that immediately when these faculty are put on the tenure track their contracts should include this expectation. Service expectations should be described in detail in the contract. Because one goal of these changes is to better integrate this group of faculty, all service expectations should include attendance at department meetings. Other expectations to be determined after a greater understanding of the different cultures that currently exist across campus.

What differences will there be between faculty who are converted to TT Senior Instructor positions and those newly hired into those positions?

While faculty who are converted will have 3 years to prepare their tenure cases before the up-or-out moment, the track for new hires will be the same as what is currently in place, with the tenure decision happening during the 6th year of employment.

How will Senior Instructors be evaluated for tenure?

We recommend that this evaluation be carried out by tenured faculty only. In the past, non-tenure-track faculty could argue that they should be evaluated by their "peers." This was akin to junior tenure-track faculty evaluating each other. Within the new system, a senior, tenured cohort will be available to evaluate junior instructors.

Bibliography

"1915 Declaration of Principles on Academic Freedom and Academic Tenure." Appendix I, *AAUP Policy Documents and Reports*. 11th ed. Washington, DC: American Association of University Professors, 2006.

Anderson, Amanda. "Cryptonormativism and Double Gestures: Reconceiving Poststructuralist Social Theory," *Cultural Critique* 21 (1992): 63–95.

——— *The Way We Argue Now: A Study in the Cultures of Theory*. Princeton University Press, 2006.

Anderson, L. V. "Death of a Professor," *Slate* 17 Nov. 2013. http://www.slate.com/articles/news_and_politics/education/2013/11/death_of_duquesne_adjunct_margaret_mary_vojtko_what_really_happened_to_her.html

Arendt, Hannah. *Between Past and Future*. New York: Viking, 1961.

——— *The Human Condition*. University of Chicago Press, 1958.

——— *The Last Interview and Other Conversations*. New York: Melville House, 2013.

——— *The Origins of Totalitarianism*. New York: Harcourt Brace Jovanovich, 1973 [1951].

Aronowitz, Stanley. *The Last Good Job in America: Work and Education in the New Global Technoculture*. Lanham, MD: Rowman and Littlefield, 2001.

Baker, Beth. "The End of the Academy?" *BioScience* 64.8 (2014): 647–652. http://bioscience.oxfordjournals.org/content/64/8/647.full

Bauerlein, Mark. "English's Self-Inflicted Wounds," *Chronicle of Higher Education* 31 May 2013. http://chronicle.com/blogs/conversation/2013/05/31/englishs-self-inflicted-wounds/

Baynton, Douglas. "Disability and the Justification of Inequality in U.S. History." In Paul K. Longmore and Lauri Umansky, eds. *The New Disability History: American Perspectives*. New York University Press, 2001. 33–57.

Benhabib, Seyla, Judith Butler, Drucilla Cornell, and Nancy Fraser. *Feminist Contentions: A Philosophical Exchange*. New York: Routledge, 1995.

Berry, Joe. *Reclaiming the Ivory Tower: Organizing Adjuncts to Change Higher Education*. New York: Monthly Review Press, 2005.

Bibliography

Bérubé, Michael. "Among the Majority," *Modern Language Association: From the President* 1 Feb. 2012. http://www.mla.org/fromthepres&topic=146

—— "Breaking News: Humanities in Decline! Film at 11," 16 Nov. 2010. http://crookedtimber.org/2010/11/16/breaking-news-humanities-in-decline-film-at-11/

—— *The Employment of English: Theory, Jobs, and the Future of Literary Studies*. New York University Press, 1998.

—— *The Left At War*. New York University Press, 2009.

—— *Public Access: Literary Theory and American Cultural Politics*. New York: Verso, 1994.

—— *Rhetorical Occasions: Essays on Humans and the Humanities*. Chapel Hill: University of North Carolina Press, 2006.

—— *What's Liberal about the Liberal Arts? Classroom Politics and "Bias" in Higher Education*. New York: W. W. Norton, 2006.

Bérubé, Michael and Cary Nelson, eds. *Higher Education Under Fire: Politics, Economics, and the Crisis of the Humanities*. New York: Routledge, 1995.

Bok, Derek. *Higher Education in America*. Princeton University Press, 2013.

Boldt, Josh. "99 Problems But Tenure Ain't One," *Chronicle Vitae (Chronicle of Higher Education)* 21 Jan. 2014. https://chroniclevitae.com/news/283-99-problems-but-tenure-ain-t-one

—— "Crowdsourcing a Compilation of Adjunct Working Conditions," *Order of Education* 2 Feb. 2012. http://orderofeducation.com/crowdsourcing-a-compilation-of-adjunct-working-conditions/

—— "Free-Market Faculty Members," *Profession 2013*. New York: Modern Language Association. http://profession.commons.mla.org/2013/10/08/free-market-faculty-members/

Bousquet, Marc. *How the University Works: Higher Education and the Low-Wage Nation*. New York University Press, 2008.

—— "The Waste Product of Graduate Education: Toward a Dictatorship of the Flexible," *Social Text* 20.1 (2002): 81–104.

Brooks, David. "The Humanist Vocation," *New York Times*, 20 Jun. 2013. http://www.nytimes.com/2013/06/21/opinion/brooks-the-humanist-vocation.html?_r=0

Burgan, Mary. *What Ever Happened to the Faculty? Drift and Decision in Higher Education*. Baltimore: Johns Hopkins University Press, 2006.

Butler, Judith. *Gender Trouble: Feminism and the Subversion of Identity*. New York: Routledge, 1990.

Calhoun, Craig. "Academic Freedom: Public Knowledge and the Structural Transformation of the University," *Social Research* 76.2 (2009): 561–598.

Chace, William M. "The Decline of the English Department," *American Scholar* (Autumn 2009). http://theamericanscholar.org/the-decline-of-the-english-department/

Bibliography

Cohen, Patricia. "In Tough Times, the Humanities Must Justify Their Worth," *New York Times* 24 Feb. 2009. http://www.nytimes.com/2009/02/25/books/25human.html?pagewanted=all

Cross, John G., and Edie N. Goldenberg, *Off-Track Profs: Nontenured Teachers in Higher Education*. Cambridge, MA: MIT Press, 2009.

Delbanco, Andrew. "The Decline and Fall of Literature," *New York Review of Books* 4 Nov. 1999. http://www.nybooks.com/articles/archives/1999/nov/04/the-decline-and-fall-of-literature/

Del Favero, Marietta, and Nathaniel Bray. "The Faculty–Administrator Relationship: Partners in Prospective Governance?" *Scholar-Practitioner Quarterly* 3.1 (2005): 53–72.

Deresiewicz, William. "Adaptation: On Literary Darwinism," *The Nation* 20 May 2009. http://www.thenation.com/article/adaptation-literary-darwinism

——— "The Disadvantages of an Elite Education," *American Scholar* Summer 2008. http://theamericanscholar.org/the-disadvantages-of-an-elite-education/#.U-TTQPldUqs

——— *Excellent Sheep: The Miseducation of the American Elite and the Way to a Meaningful Life*. New York: Free Press, 2014.

Digest of Education Statistics. Washington, DC: National Center for Education Statistics.

"The Digital Degree," *The Economist* 28 Jun. 2104. http://www.economist.com/news/briefing/21605899-staid-higher-education-business-about-experience-welcome-earthquake-digital

Dunn, Allen. "Who Needs a Sociology of the Aesthetic? Freedom and Value in Bourdieu's *Rules of Art*," *boundary 2* 25.1 (1998): 87–110.

Editors of *Lingua Franca*. *The Sokal Hoax: The Sham that Shook the Academy*. Lincoln: University of Nebraska Press, 2000.

Ellis, John M. *Literature Lost: Social Agendas and the Corruption of the Humanities*. New Haven: Yale University Press, 1997.

——— "Poisoning the Wells of Knowledge," *New York Times* 28 Mar. 1998.

Fafblog. "Fafblog Interview Week: Fafblog Interviews Dr. James Dobson." 25 May 2004. http://fafblog.blogspot.com/2004/05/fafblog-interview-week-fafblog.html

Finkin, Matthew, and Robert Post. *For the Common Good: Principles of American Academic Freedom*. New Haven: Yale University Press, 2009.

Flaherty, Colleen. "More 'Intentionality' Needed," *Inside Higher Ed* 23 Jun. 2014. https://www.insidehighered.com/news/2014/06/23/discussion-focuses-envisioning-faculty-models-future

Frank, Thomas. "Congratulations, Class of 2014: You're Totally Screwed," *Salon* 18 May 2014. http://www.salon.com/2014/05/18/congratulations_class_of_2014_youre_totally_ screwed/

Bibliography

———. "The Trigger Warning We Need: 'College is a Scam Meant to Perpetuate the 1 Percent," *Salon* 25 May 2014. http://www.salon.com/2014/05/25/the_1_percents_college_ scam/

Fruscione, Joseph. "What Parents Need to Know About College Faculty," *PBS Newshour: Making Sen$e* 14 Aug. 2014. http://www.pbs.org/newshour/making-sense/what-parents-need-to-know-about-college-faculty/

———. "When a College Contracts 'Adjunctivitis,' It's the Students Who Lose," *PBS Newshour: Making Sen$e* 25 Jul. 2014. http://www.pbs.org/newshour/making-sense/when-a-college-contracts-adjunctivitis-its-the-students-who-lose/

Gerber, Larry G. "Professionalization as the Basis for Academic Freedom and Faculty Governance," *AAUP Journal of Academic Freedom* 1 (2010): 1–26.

Giroux, Henry. *The University in Chains: Confronting the Military-Industrial-Academic Complex*. Boulder, CO: Paradigm, 2007.

Guillory, John. *Cultural Capital: The Problem of Literary Canon Formation*. University of Chicago Press, 1993.

Habermas, Jürgen. "Modernity—An Incomplete Project." In Hal Foster, ed., *The Anti-Aesthetic: Essays on Postmodern Culture*. Seattle: Bay Press, 1983. 3–15.

Hamacher, Werner, Neil H. Hertz, and Thomas Keenan, eds. *Responses: On Paul de Man's Wartime Journalism*. Lincoln: University of Nebraska Press, 1988.

Herman, Deborah M. and Julie Schmid, eds. *Cogs in the Classroom Factory: The Changing Identity of Academic Labor*. Westport, CT: Greenwood, 2003.

House Committee on Education and the Workforce, Democratic Staff. *The Just-in-Time Professor: A Staff Report Summarizing eForum Responses on the Working Conditions of Contingent Faculty in Higher Education*. U.S. House of Representatives. Washington, DC, 2014.

The Inclusion in Governance of Faculty Members Holding Contingent Appointments. Washington, DC: American Association of University Professors, 2012. http://www.aaup.org/ report/governance-inclusion

Jaschik, Scott. "Skepticism about Tenure, MOOCs and the Presidency: A Survey of Provosts," *Inside Higher Ed* 23 Jan. 2013. https://www.insidehighered.com/news/survey/skepticism-about-tenure-moocs-and-presidency-survey-provosts

Jameson, Fredric. *The Political Unconscious: Narrative as a Socially Symbolic Act*. Ithaca: Cornell University Press, 1981.

Jay, Paul. *The Humanities "Crisis" and the Future of Literary Study*. New York: Palgrave Macmillan, 2014.

Kelsky, Karen. "Adjuncts, Assistant Professors, and a Broken Faculty Life Cycle," *The Professor Is In* (blog), 25 Jul. 2014. http://theprofessor isin.com/2014/07/25/adjuncts-assistant-professors-and-a-broken-faculty-life-cycle/

Kermode, Frank. "The Academy vs. the Humanities," *Atlantic Monthly* Aug. 1997. http://www.theatlantic.com/past/docs/issues/97aug/academy.htm

Kernan, Alvin. *The Death of Literature*. New Haven: Yale University Press, 1992.

———— ed. *What's Happened to the Humanities?* Princeton University Press, 1997.

Kimball, Roger. "The Periphery v. the Center: The MLA in Chicago," *New Criterion* 9.6 (Feb. 1991). http://www.newcriterion.com/articles.cfm/The-periphery-vs—the-center—the-MLA-in-Chicago-5411

Kittay, Eva Feder. *Love's Labor: Essays on Women, Equality, and Dependency*. New York: Routledge, 1999.

Klinkenborg, Verlyn. "The Decline and Fall of the English Major," *New York Times* 22 Jun. 2013. http://www.nytimes.com/2013/06/23/opinion/sunday/the-decline-and-fall-of-the-english-major.html?_r=0

Kovalik, Daniel. "Death of an Adjunct," *Pittsburgh Post-Gazette* 18 Sept. 2013. http://www.post-gazette.com/opinion/Op-Ed/2013/09/18/Death-of-an-adjunct/stories/201309180224

Landers, Elizabeth. "Contingent Labor: National Perspectives, Local Solutions," *Profession 2013*. http://profession.commons.mla.org/2013/10/08/contingent-labor-national-perspectives-local-solutions/

Laurence, David. "A Profile of the Non-Tenure-Track Academic Workforce," *ADE (Association of Departments of English) Bulletin* 153 (2014): 6–22.

Leatherman, Courtney, and Robin Wilson. "Embittered by a Bleak Job Market, Graduate Students Take on the MLA," 18 Dec. 1998. https://chronicle.com/article/Embittered-by-a-Bleak-Job/30852

Lehman, David. *Signs of the Times: Deconstruction and the Fall of Paul de Man*. New York: Poseidon Press, 1991.

Leo, John. "Campus Life, Fully Exposed," *U.S. News and World Report* 10 Jan. 2005. Rpt. http://wesleyanargus.com/2005/01/25/campus-life-fully-exposed/

Levi, Edward H. *Point of View: Talks on Education*. University of Chicago Press, 1970.

Levine, George. "Putting the 'Literature' Back into Literature Departments," *ADE Bulletin* 113 (1996): 13–20.

Longmate, Jack, and Frank Cosco. *Program for Change: 2010–2030*. Revised, 2013. http://vccfa.ca/newsite/wp-content/uploads/2012/05/Access-the-Program-for-Change-May-2013.pdf

Marshall, Thurgood. "Remarks of Thurgood Marshall at the Annual Seminar of the San Francisco Patent and Trade Law Association,"

Maui, Hawaii, 6 May 1987. http://www.thurgoodmarshall.com/speeches/constitutional_speech.htm

McCarthy, Colman. "Adjunct Professors Fight for Crumbs on Campus," *Washington Post* 22 Aug. 2014. http://www.washingtonpost.com/opinions/adjunct-professors-fight-for-crumbs-on-campus/2014/08/22/ca92eb38-28b1-11e4-8593-da634b334390_story.html

McMahan, Jeff. "Cognitive Disability and Cognitive Enhancement." In Eva Feder Kittay and Licia Carlson, eds, *Cognitive Disability and its Challenge to Moral Philosophy*. Boston: Wiley-Blackwell, 2010. 345–367.

——— "Cognitive Disability, Misfortune, and Justice," *Philosophy and Public Affairs* 25.1 (1996): 3–35.

——— *The Ethics of Killing: Problems at the Margins of Life*. Oxford University Press, 2003.

Mehaffy, George L. "Challenge and Change," *Educause Review Online* 5 Sept. 2012. http://www.educause.edu/ero/article/challenge-and-change

Menand, Louis, ed. *The Future of Academic Freedom*. University of Chicago Press, 1996.

——— *The Metaphysical Club: A Story of Ideas in America*. New York: Farrar, Straus and Giroux, 2001.

Meranze, Michael. "We Wish We Weren't in Kansas Anymore: An Elegy for Academic Freedom," *Los Angeles Review of Books* 4 Mar. 2014. http://lareviewofbooks.org/essay/wish-werent-kansas-anymore-elegy-academic-freedom

Nelson, Cary. *No University is an Island: Saving Academic Freedom*. New York University Press, 2010.

Newfield, Christopher. *Unmaking the Public University: The Forty-Year Assault on the Middle Class*. Cambridge, MA: Harvard University Press, 2008.

Nussbaum, Martha. *Frontiers of Justice: Disability, Nationality, Species Membership*. Cambridge, MA: Harvard University Press, 2006.

Patton, Stacey. "The Ph.D. Now Comes with Food Stamps." *Chronicle of Higher Education* 6 May 2012. http://chronicle.com/article/From-Graduate-School-to/131795/

Perry, David. "Faculty Refuse to See Themselves as Workers. Why?" *Chronicle of Higher Education,* Vitae *blog*, 22 May 2104. https://chroniclevitae.com/news/509-faculty-refuse-to-see-themselves-as-workers-why

Poch, Robert. *Academic Freedom in American Higher Education: Rights, Responsibilities, and Limitations*. San Francisco: Jossey-Bass, 1993.

Post, Robert. "The Structure of Academic Freedom." In Beshara Doumani, ed., *Academic Freedom after September 11*. New York: Zone Books, 2006.

Professional Employment Practices for Non-Tenure-Track Faculty Members: Recommendations and Evaluative Questions. MLA Committee on

Contingent Labor in the Profession. New York: Modern Language Association, 2011. http://www.mla.org/pdf/clip_stmt_final_may11.pdf

"Ramifications of the Supreme Court's Ruling in Garcetti v. Ceballos," Modern Language Association Committee on Academic Freedom and Professional Rights and Responsibilities. http://www.mla.org/garcetti_ceballos

Rawls, John. *A Theory of Justice.* Cambridge, MA: Harvard University Press, 1971.

Readings, Bill. *The University in Ruins.* Cambridge, MA: Harvard University Press, 1996.

Robbins, Bruce. "Outside Pressures," *Works and Days* 51/52, 53/54 (2008–9): 339–345.

Russo, Richard. *Straight Man.* New York: Vintage, 1997.

Ruth, Jennifer. *Novel Professions: Interested Disinterest and the Making of the Professional in the Victorian Novel.* Columbus: Ohio State University Press, 2006.

―――― "What Can We Do Now that Adjunct Sections are Written Into Universities' Fiscal Survival Strategy?" *Remaking the University* 22 Jul. 2014. http://utotherescue.blogspot.com/2014/07/what-can-we-do-now-that-adjunct.html

―――― "When Tenure-Track Faculty Take on the Problem of Adjunctification," *Remaking the University* 25 May 2013. http://utotherescue.blogspot.com/2013/05/when-tenure-track-faculty-take-on.html

―――― "Why Are Faculty Complicit in Creating a Disposable Workforce?" *Remaking the University* 13 Jul. 2014. http://utotherescue.blogspot.com/2014/07/why-are-faculty-complicit-in-creating.html

Samuels, Robert. *Why Public Higher Education Should Be Free: How to Decrease Cost and Increase Quality at American Universities.* New Brunswick, NJ: Rutgers University Press, 2013.

Schmidt, Ben. "A Crisis in the Humanities?" *Chronicle of Higher Education* 10 Jun. 2013. http://chronicle.com/blognetwork/edgeofthewest/2013/06/10/the-humanities-crisis/

Schmidt, Peter. "New Complaint to Accreditor Assails College's Treatment of Adjuncts," *Chronicle of Higher Education* 17 Apr. 2013. http://chronicle.com/article/New-Complaint-to-Accreditor/138555

Schumacher, Julie. *Dear Committee Members.* New York: Doubleday, 2014.

Scott, Joan Wallach. "Knowledge, Power, and Academic Freedom," *Social Research* 76.2 (2009): 451–480.

Segran, Elizabeth. "The Adjunct Revolt: How Poor Professors Are Fighting Back," *Atlantic* 28 Apr. 2014. http://www.theatlantic.com/business/archive/2014/04/the-adjunct-professor-crisis/361336/2/

Silver, Nate. "As More Attend College, Majors Become More Career-Focused," *New York Times* 25 Jun. 2013. http://fivethirtyeight.blogs.nytimes.com/2013/06/25/as-more-attend-college-majors-become-more-career-focused

Singer, Peter. *Rethinking Life and Death: The Collapse of our Traditional Ethics*. New York: St. Martin's, 1994.

——— "Speciesism and Moral Status." In Eva Feder Kittay and Licia Carlson, eds, *Cognitive Disability and its Challenge to Moral Philosophy*. Boston: Wiley-Blackwell, 2010. 331–344.

Small, Helen. *The Value of the Humanities*. Oxford University Press, 2013.

Smith, Barbara Herrnstein. *Contingencies of Value: Alternative Perspectives for Critical Theory*. Cambridge, MA: Harvard University Press, 1988.

Staton, Michael. "The Degree is Doomed," *Harvard Business Review HBR Blog Network*, 8 Jan. 2014. http://blogs.hbr.org/2014/01/the-degree-is-doomed/

Swarns, Rachel L. "Crowded Out of Ivory Tower, Adjuncts See a Life Less Lofty," *New York Times* 19 Jan. 2014. http://www.nytimes.com/2014/01/20/nyregion/crowded-out-of-ivory-tower-adjuncts-see-a-life-less-lofty.html?_r=0

The Teaching of the Arts and Humanities at Harvard College: Mapping the Future. http://artsandhumanities.fas.harvard.edu/files/humanities/files/mapping_the_future_31_may_2013.pdf

Tenure and Teaching-Intensive Appointments. Washington, DC: American Association of University Professors, 2009. http://www.aaup.org/report/tenure-and-teaching-intensive-appointments

Veblen, Thorstein. *The Higher Learning in America: A Memorandum on the Conduct of Universities by Business Men*. New York: Cosimo, 2005 [1904].

Index

Bold entries refer to figures or tables.

academic freedom, 24
  contingent faculty, 12, 15, 104
  "Declaration of Principles
    on Academic Freedom and
    Academic Tenure" (1915),
    101–102, 113
  different conceptions of, 87–88
  Garcetti v. Ceballos (United
    States Supreme Court),
    107–109
  loss of, 110–111
  negative version of, 106–107,
    109–110
  as paradoxical principle, 114
  as a professional freedom,
    101–102, 105, 109, 116
  radical nature of, 114
  reconceptualized in terms of
    rights, 104–105
  shared governance, 89, 107,
    114
  tenure system, 101–103,
    114–115
academic infighting, 89–90
accountability
  administration/administrators,
    80
  tenured faculty, 75–76, 127,
    128
  universities, 138
activism of contingent faculty,
  62–64, 121–124, 125
  attitudes toward tenure,
    124–125

Adjunct Action, 63
adjunct faculty, 13
  invisibility of, 16
  lack of stake in institutions,
    88
  original function of, 17
  as permanent feature, 83
  wages, 60–61, 122–123
  years spent teaching, 16–17
  see also contingent faculty
Adjunct Faculty Association,
  121–122
Adjunct Project, 122–123
administration/administrators
  accountability, 80
  attitudes toward tenure, 78–79,
    80
  denial over contingent faculty
    system, 130
  expansion of, 22, 76–77
  pressures on, 79, 82
  tensions with faculty, 79,
    82
Albert, David, 51
American Academy of Arts and
  Sciences, *The Heart of the
  Matter*, 1
American Association of
  University Professors, 12, 13,
  24–25, 135
  "Declaration of Principles
    on Academic Freedom and
    Academic Tenure" (1915),
    101–102, 113

Index

American Association of University Professors – *continued*
  The Inclusion in Governance of Faculty Members Holding Contingent Appointments, 111, 112, 113, 115, 118
  "On the Relationship of Faculty Governance to Academic Freedom," 107
  "Statement of Principles on Academic Freedom and Tenure" (1940), 102, 106
  Tenure and Teaching-Intensive Appointments, 88, 117, 126, 129–130
American Federation of Teachers (AFT), 63
Amnesty International, 36
Anderson, Amanda, 38
animal rights, 34, 40, 45, 46
Arendt, Hannah, 102, 103, 114, 117–118
Aronowitz, Stanley, 57

Bauerlein, Mark, 2
Baynton, Douglas, 47
Benhabib, Seyla, 35
Berlin, Isaiah, 106
Berry, Joe, 60, 88, 121
Bok, Derek, 127–128
Boldt, Josh, 81, 122–123, 124–125
Bousquet, Marc, 16, 20, 57, 129, 134–135
Brooks, David, 1–2
Burgan, Mary, 89
Butler, Judith, 34
  universalism, 35–37, 38

Calhoun, Craig, 109
Ceballos, Richard, 107–108
Chace, William M., 2, 3–4
Coalition of Contingent Academic Labor (COCAL), 121

cognitive capacity, 40, 45
  and moral status, 43–44, 45–46
Cohen, Patricia, 27
Conley, Valerie Martin, 83–84
contingency, 33–34
  contextual nature of value, 33
  human rights, 34
contingent faculty, 12, 13
  attitudes toward tenure, 104, 124–125
  converting to teaching-intensive tenured positions, 19–20: evaluation for tenure, 149; evaluation of teaching, 147; impact of reform on, 136, 144–145; Portland State University, 142–148; privileging of PhD holders, 134–135; service workload, 148
  costs of reform, 134
  courseloads, 91–92
  dependence on department head, 88
  as employment choice, 18–19
  expansion of, 111
  failed strategy of converting to tenure lines, 67–69
  "freeway flyers," 18
  growth across disciplines, 129–130
  ineligibility for unemployment benefits, 15
  institutional designation of, 17
  lack of academic freedom, 12, 15, 104
  need for reform of hiring process, 94–95
  not treated as professionals, 130–131
  number of, 14
  participation in governance: consequences of, 112; erosion

of tenure, 99–101; problems with, 115–116; weak position in, 98–99, 111–112
patronage systems, 92–93, 94
perceptions of, 17
powerlessness of, 123
precarious position of, 18, 103
problems with reforming non-tenure track policy, 95–98
shared governance, 101
tenure as long-term solution for, 126
unequal access to promotion, 95–96
wages, 14–15, 17, 122–123
see also activism of contingent faculty; adjunct faculty
Cosco, Frank, 139n
Cross, John, 90
cultural capital, devaluation of, 58–59
culture wars, 8–9

decision-making, academic, 95
contingent faculty's participation in, 98, 101
"Declaration of Principles on Academic Freedom and Academic Tenure" (1915), 101–102, 113
Delbanco, Andrew, 4–5, 27, 28
de Man, Paul, 51
democracy, 101, 115
deprofessionalization of college teaching, 11, 14
activism in combating, 62–64, 121–124
consequences of, 11–12, 70–71
impact on graduate programs, 16
inertia of tenured faculty, 64–71: advantages of adjunct hiring, 66–67; feelings of helplessness, 64–65; hoping to convert to tenure lines, 67–69; innocence of, 66; institutional costs, 69–71; personal costs, 69
tenure as long-term solution for, 126
Deresiewicz, William, 49–50, 137
Dewey, John, 114
disability studies
cognitive capacity, 44, 45
Down syndrome, 40–43
general relevance of, 47–48
inequality, 47
philosophy's silence on disability, 40
universalism, 39
doctorate (PhD), *see* terminal degrees
Down syndrome, 40–43

Enlightenment
critique of, 30, 32–33
as incomplete project, 38
universality, 30

Feal, Rosemary, 64
Fish, Stanley, 51
Frank, Thomas, 71, 76
"freeway flyers," 18
Fruscione, Joe, 121

Gerber, Larry, 101, 107, 115
Giroux, Henry, 79
Goldenberg, Edie, 90
governance
contingent faculty's participation in, 12: consequences of, 112; erosion of tenure, 99–101; problems with, 115–116; weak position of, 98–99, 111–112
tenured faculty's participation in, 75, 77
see also shared governance

graduate programs, impact of deprofessionalization, 16
Green River Community College, 98–99
Greenstadt, Amy, 14, 132
Guillory, John, 58, 59, 60, 61

Habermas, Jürgen, 37–38, 40
Hall, Tamron, 2
Harvard, 7
Harvey, David, 58
Heraclitus, 30
higher education, 138–139
  achievements of American system, 137–138
  decline in funding of, 15–16, 22
  erosion of, 138
  inequality in, 24
  university's mission, 24–25
hiring of faculty
  expansion of non-tenure faculty, 90–91
  fast-tracked hiring, 91
  growth of patronage system, 92–93, 94
  inequality in courseloads, 91–92
  need to reform contingent faculty hiring, 94–95: problems with, 95–98
  teaching-intensive tenure track, 146–147: evaluation of teaching, 147
  tenured faculty, 93, 94
  terminal degrees, 19–20, 134–135
  three-tiered system, 90
  unprofessional practices, 19, 20
Hoeller, Keith, 98–99
Hoff, J. D., 121
homophobia, 34–35
House Committee on Education and the Workforce, 63

humanities
  attacks on current practices in, 3, 4–5, 14, 49–50
  aversion to timelessness and universality, 29, 30
  calls for justification of, 27–28
  decline in tenure-track jobs, 10, 15, 60
  decline narrative, 1–5, 7: reasons for, 9–10
  degrees as percentage of all degrees, **4**
  degrees as percentage of college-age population, **6**
  employment crisis, 58
  impact of socio-economic changes, 58, 59–60, 61
  increase in degrees awarded in, 5–7
  justification of, 51–54
  public image of, 50–51
  self-inflicted wounds, 49, 50–51
  stability of undergraduate enrollments, 7–8
  traditional justification for, 29
human rights, contingent nature of, 34

ideology, claims of universality, 30
inequality
  disability, 47
  higher education, 24
Instructor Bill of Rights, 103, 111

Jameson, Fredric, 30
Johnson, Barbara, 51

Kelsky, Karen, 78–79
Kennedy, Anthony, 108
Kermode, Frank, 5
Kezar, Adrianna, 130
Kimball, Roger, 34

Index

Kittay, Eva, 39, 40
Klinkenborg, Verlyn, 7
Kronman, Arthur, 27

Landers, Elizabeth, 123, 136
Lehman, David, 33
Leo, John, 34
Levi, Edward, 23–24
Levine, George, 58–59, 60
literary studies, attacks on current practices in, 49–50
Lloyd, Curtis, 83
Longmate, Jack, 139n
Lovejoy, Arthur, 101–102, 114
Lyotard, Jean-François, 37, 38

Maisto, Maria, 63, 121, 123
managerial staff, expansion of, 22
Marshall, Thurgood, 30, 31–32, 40
McCarthy, Colman, 121
McMahan, Jeff, 43–44, 45–46, 47
Menand, Louis, 75, 93, 116
Meranze, Michael, 12, 88, 110–111
Miller, George, 63
modernity, as incomplete project, 40
Modern Language Association (MLA), 12, 17, 63, 107, 122, 123, 135
  Professional Employment Practices for Non-Tenure Track Faculty Members, 131–132
moral status, and cognitive capacity, 43–44, 45–46

National Center for Education Statistics, 7
National Study of Postsecondary Faculty, 16
Nelson, Cary, 57, 77, 114
New Faculty Majority (NFM), 63, 121, 122–123

Newfield, Christopher, 8–9, 12
Nussbaum, Martha, 39

Oakley, Francis C., 27

Part-Time Worker Bill of Rights Act (2013), 63
patronage systems, 89, 115–116
  growth of, 92–93, 94
peer review
  teaching-intensive tenured positions, 19
  tenured faculty, 13, 17, 88
Penn State University, 13
Perry, David, 81
philosophy, and disability, 40
Poch, Robert, 80
political correctness, 34
Portland State University (PSU), 14, 84–85
  Ad Hoc Committee on NTT Faculty Policy, 95–96, 128
  casualization of faculty, 129
  Curriculum Committee, 96–97
  implementing teaching-intensive tenure track, 142–148: evaluation for tenure, 148; evaluation of teaching, 147, 148; hiring process, 146–147; impact on contingent faculty, 144–145; reasons for, 143–144
  problems with reforming non-tenure track policy, 95–98
  salary minimums, 132, **133**
Poston, Muriel, 130
Post, Robert, 104–105, 114
private universities, increase in tuition costs, 22
privatization, impact on public universities, 8–9
professional associations, combating deprofessionalization, 63
promotion, unequal access to, 95–96

161

Index

public universities
   distinctive features of, 8–9
   increase in tuition costs, 15, 21–22
   loss of trust in, 71
   see also higher education

queer theory, 34–35

Rawls, John, 39
Reading, Bill, 57
Reed, Adolph, Jr., 39
Re, Kathryn, 98
relativism, 33
Robbins, Bruce, 116
Ross, Andrew, 51
Ruhl, Nathan, 129–130
Russo, Richard, 65

Samuels, Robert, 121, 123
Schmid, Julie, 57
Schmidt, Ben, 5–6
Schumacher, Julie, 62, 64–65
Scott, Joan, 116
Sedgwick, Eve, 34
Seligman, Edwin, 101–102
Service Employees International Union (SEIU), 63
shared governance, 77–78
   academic freedom, 89, 107, 114
   academic infighting, 89–90
   deterioration of, 89
   equality through organization, 114
   rewarding nature of, 106
   tensions in, 79
   tenured faculty, 101–103
   see also governance
Silver, Nate, 5
Sinclair, Upton, 112
Singer, Peter, 40–41, 42, 43–44, 47
Small, Helen, 11
Smith, Barbara Herrnstein, 30, 33

social constructionism, 42–43
social contract tradition, critique of, 39
Sokal hoax, 51
Souter, David, 108
Sowards, Robin, 121
speciesism, 44
student debt, 22, 71

teaching-intensive tenure track, 19
   benefits of, 75–76
   costs of reform, 134
   evaluation for tenure, 148
   evaluation of teaching, 147
   hiring process, 146–147
   impact of reform on contingent faculty, 136, 144–145
   local variations in reform process, 136–137
   need for, 129–130
   privileging of PhD holders, 19–20, 134–135
   proposal for implementation at Portland State University, 142–148
   reasons for, 143–144
   service workload, 148
tenured faculty/system
   academic freedom, 101–103, 114–115
   accountability, 75–76, 127, 128
   contingent faculty's attitude toward, 104, 124–125
   courseloads, 91
   decline in, 10, 15, 60
   defense of, 127–128
   empowerment of, 126–127
   equality, 90, 117
   erosion of tenure, 99–101
   expansion through changes in division of labor, 72–74

hiring process, 93, 94
independence, 72, 74–75, 117–118, 126–127
inertia in face of deprofessionalization, 64–71: advantages of adjunct hiring, 66–67; denial over, 130; feelings of helplessness, 64–65; hoping to convert to tenure lines, 67–69; innocence over, 66; institutional costs, 69–71; personal costs, 69
institutional designation of, 17–18
as long-term solution for contingent faculty, 126
opposition to tenure system, 23, 127
participation in university governance, 75
peer review, 13, 17, 88
professional identity, 82
public's view of, 71
responsibilities of, 82
self-perceptions, 81–82
tensions with administrators, 79, 80, 82
tenure as legitimating concept, 75, 93, 113–114
see also teaching-intensive tenure track
terminal degrees
alleged overproduction of PhDs, 16
hiring of faculty, 19–20
privileging holders of, 134–135
underhiring of PhDs, 135
TIAA-CREF (Teachers Insurance and Annuity Association—College Retirement Equities Fund), 83

timelessness
critique of, 29, 30
ideological motives, 30
tuition costs, 15, 20–21

undergraduate enrollment, growth in, 15
United States Constitution, 30–32
United States Supreme Court, and Garcetti v. Ceballos, 107–109
universality
critique of, 29, 30
disputes over boundaries of, 47
Enlightenment, 32–33
ideological motives, 30
as incomplete project, 38–39
Judith Butler on, 35–37, 38
openness to challenge, 40, 46–47
poststructuralist critique of, 46–47
University of California-American Federation of Teachers, 121

value, contextual nature of, 33
Vancouver Plan, 139n
Veblen, Thorstein, 110
visual and performing arts, degrees awarded, 6–7
Vojtko, Margaret Mary, 16–17, 121

wages
adjunct faculty, 60–61
Adjunct Project, 122–123
contingent faculty, 14–15, 122–123
minimum recommendations, 17
Portland State faculty, 132, **133**
Vancouver Plan, 139n
Warner, Michael, 34

Yaboski, Paul, 83
Yale, 7

Printed and bound by CPI Group (UK) Ltd, Croydon, CR0 4YY